# PHARISEES

## Friend or Foe?

A BE KY Book ©

Hollisa Alewine, PhD

# DEDICATION

To those rabbis, Hebrew tutors, scholars, and friends who have patiently guided me through the Jewish sources.

# CONTENTS

# GLOSSARY

**Adonai** – My Lord.

**Aggadah** – An illustrative story that may use Biblical characters to teach a lesson, but the story is not found in Scripture.

**Am Ha-Aretz** – Commoners, or People of the Land. It was not a compliment. Some scholars believe that the derogatory phrase was reserved for Galileans, but others say it applied to any Jew, commoner or priest, who rejected the additional Oral Law fences of purity.

**Bat kol** – "Daughter voice," a Divine voice from Heaven. An example is when Yeshua is immersed by John, and a Divine voice says, "This is my Beloved Son, in whom I am well-pleased."

**Eden** – delight or pleasure.

**Erev Shabbat** – The eve of Shabbat that starts at sundown on Friday evenings.

**Elohim** – God the Creator.

**Eschatology** – A branch of theology that discusses the events that lie at the very end of history and of time as we know and experience it.

**Ethnocentricism** - The attitude that one's own group, ethnicity, or nationality is superior to others.

**False dilemma** – Oversimplification that offers a limited number of options (usually two) when in reality more options are available. A false dilemma arises when a trap is set to convince someone that there are two and only two mutually exclusive options, when that is untrue. Often one of the options is unacceptable and repulsive, while the other is the one the manipulator wants us to choose. Examples: "Are you a Republican or a Democrat?" "Do you support tax increases, or are you stingy?"

**Halakha** – Jewish law and jurisprudence, based on the Talmud. It describes how Israel will "walk" out the commandments, for the word is formed from the Hebrew verb *halakh*, walk.

**Hasid(im) or Chasidim** – Pious; pious ones.

**Hasty Generalization** – A hasty generalization draws a general rule from atypical cases.

**Hermeneutics** - Methods of Biblical interpretation applying accepted rules of interpretation.

**Kohen/Kohen HaGadol** – Priest/High Priest.

**Logical fallacy** – A logical fallacy is an error of reasoning. When someone adopts a position, or tries to persuade someone else to adopt a position, based on a bad piece of reasoning, it is a manipulation of thought.

**Mikveh/Mikvaot** – Ritual bath/baths required by both Torah and Jewish law.

**Minchag** – An accepted tradition or group of traditions in Judaism observed by a community and unique to that community.

**Mishnah or "Oral Torah"** – The Jewish oral law traditionally believed to have been passed down from Moses. Yeshua usually upheld the oral law of the House of Hillel, but he overruled most of the oral laws of the House of Shammai. They were the two predominant schools of the Pharisees in the First Century.

**Mitzvah** – Commandment.

**Oneg** – delight, pleasure one should derive from celebrating Shabbat.

**Pejorative** – A word or phrase that has negative connotations or that is intended to disparage or belittle.

**Proto-rabbis** – religious teachers of the pre-Mishnaic period, a time when the designation "rabbi" existed, but was used less as an identification as the later period. The later rabbinic period emerged from the multiple sects of First Century Judaism. Yeshua was sometimes called "Rabbi," so the title was used in the proto-rabbinic period.

**Pseudepigrapha** – "Fake name." Any of various pseudonymous or anonymous Jewish religious writings of the period 200 b.c. to a.d. 200; such writings are not included in any canon of biblical Scripture.

**Rebbe/Rabbi** – A Jewish spiritual leader or teacher.

**Ruach HaKodesh** - Holy Spirit.

**Stereotype** – Standardized mental picture that is held in common by members of a group and that represents an oversimplified opinion, prejudiced attitude, or uncritical judgment. By "uncritical judgment," the definition means that the mental picture is not subjected to logical, analytical standards of judgment.

**Talmud** – The largest body of Jewish law and commentary containing the Mishnah, Gemara, and Tosefta.

**TANAKH** – Old Testament. Tanakh is an acronym for Torah, Neviim, Ketuvim, or Law, Prophets, and Writings, the ancient divisions of the Hebrew Bible. The books of the Tanakh are the same as, but are not arranged in the same order as Christian Bibles.

**Torah** – The first five books of the Bible, misunderstood as "law" in English translations. The Torah is more accurately God's teaching and instruction. It contains topics such as science, history, priestly procedures, civil statutes, ordinances, health, agriculture, commandments, prophecies, prayer, animal husbandry, architecture, civics, and many others. The root word of Torah comes from the Hebrew word *yarah*, which means "to hit the mark." Torah may also be used to refer to all of the Hebrew Bible, or even to its smallest meaning, a procedure. Torah may be used by Messianic Jews to refer to the entire Bible from Genesis to Revelation, for the Torah is the foundation for all the Scriptures. The Prophets point Israel back to the Torah. The Psalms teach one to love the Torah as King David loved it. The Writings teach the consequences of departing from the Torah and the rewards for returning to it. The New Testament brings the Torah to its fullest meaning in the person Yeshua the Messiah, and much of the New Testament quotes the Tanakh.

**World to Come (Olam Haba)** – The world of eternity beyond Messiah's 1,000-year reign.

**Yeshua** – Jesus' Hebrew name; salvation.

# 1

## THE VITAL COMMUNITY

Hypocrite. Mean. Selfish. Proud. These are the words the modern world associates with a Pharisee. While the word Pharisee has evolved to mean such negative things today, the Bible student's question is more likely, "What was a Pharisee in the time that Jesus lived?" After all, it is First Century texts that the student wants to understand so that she can put the words of the Gospels into their historical context. A Bible student doesn't want to know what a Pharisee is today.

To define a Biblical Pharisee, it is important to put him in the context of the Bible that governed every aspect of his life, the TANAKH, which is the Torah, Prophets, and Writings. It is what Christians know today as the Old Testament. The Torah is the foundational text upon which the Prophets and Writings rest, and much of the New Testament either quotes directly from or alludes to the Torah: Genesis, Exodus, Leviticus, Numbers, and Deuteronomy.

The written Torah,[1] the first five books of the Bible, is covenant between Adonai[2] and His People Israel. By its nature, a covenant joins two parties in agreement. When one considers that Israel is a people group, and therefore a community, the written Torah is a covenant that must be lived by that community. Hundreds of thousands, or even millions, of people in Israel could have observed those written commandments with just as many thousands of applications.

To prevent such chaos, judges were appointed and instructed by Moses in order to define how each tribe would interpret and apply those standards. These judges were appointed even before the building of the Tabernacle in the wilderness.[3] The message for the community is that fair and peaceful person-to-person relationships pave the way for corporate worship.

Could there have been different applications than those chosen? Of course, but to maintain order within a covenant community, standards were set. Those standards were handed down from generation to generation and became part of an oral tradition[4] known as the Oral Law. In a lecture, one modern rabbi likened the "Oral Torah" to "the user's manual for the [written] Torah."

The written Torah itself refers to the development of unwritten customs associated with its commandments. A narrative, not just a specific commandment, suggests Israelite traditions. An example is the custom of Israelites not to eat the meat of an animal with the sciatic nerve still attached. This was developed, says the Torah, in remembrance of the limp with which their ancestor Israel walked after his all-night wrestling match with the angel.[5]

The Torah's commandments are simple, but simple does not translate to its community as practical or clear. For instance, Israel is commanded not

1. For a full definition of "Torah," see BEKY Book, *What is the Torah?* by the author.

2. A name of God that means "My Lord"

3. Ex 18:21-23

4. For more detailed historical and analytical discussions of the "Oral Law," see S. Creeger's *Introduction to the Jewish Sources* and the author's *Truth, Tradition, or Tare? Growing in the Word.*

5. Ge 32:32

to kindle a fire on the Sabbath[6] (*Shabbat*); they are to rest on that day. What constitutes "rest" is debatable. A hint is that prior to Shabbat, Israelites are to "bake what you will bake and boil what you will boil"[7] in preparation, presumably so that they will eat the cooked food on Shabbat and not kindle a fire to prepare meals. How to keep that cooked food warm throughout Shabbat was a question tackled by the Oral Law and local community custom, called *minchag*.

There is a Biblical example of how individuals must test whether their practices are freedom of worship or spiritual rebellion. A man found picking up sticks to kindle a fire on Shabbat[8] eventually was put to death after trial, for there is no evidence of repentance. Since the stick-collector was free to leave the community at any time once he heard the Ten Commandments, his behavior was intended to force his own interpretation of Shabbat upon the entire community. Perhaps the stick collector said to himself, "Well, I won't cook on Shabbat, but I will gather sticks for cooking. This is my personal interpretation."

After Moses inquired of the Lord, the ruling was no, don't even *prepare* to bake or boil once Shabbat begins by picking up sticks to do so. It gives the appearance of evil intent. It's not rest, and ultimately every commandment of the Torah prophesies of Messiah Yeshua (Jesus) in some way. Individuals may not impose their unique interpretations of the Torah upon the community, only qualified, appointed judges. There are other opportunities to express one's individuality, but God did not permit open rebellion.

The gathering action signaled both the intent to violate the Shabbat commandment (the appearance of evil) as well as violation of carrying burdens[9] on Shabbat, a form of creative or commercial work. These situations in the ancient text

6. Ex 35:3

7. Ex 16:23

8. Nu 15:32

9. Je 17:22, 24

13

demanded clarification. A clarification in Hebrew is a *pirush*, or commentary that lends understanding. From this noun one hears the same root as *Parush*, or Pharisee.

The Pharisees emerged as a group of scholars who studied the Biblical text in order to clarify it for the common person and the community to whom the text was the final authority, yet they needed practical insight. Practical applications arise from real-life problems. In the fire-kindling prohibition, however, implicit in the commandment is a desire for the entire community to delight in the day spent focused on their prophetic engagement and fellowship with their Creator. The Creation was a delightful thing, and obedience was intended for Israel both to remember and look forward to Shabbat in the Presence of Elohim (God).

This need for clarification is often found in the Prophets and Writings, which the Pharisees diligently studied alongside the Torah text. What is commanded, but not descriptive, in the most ancient document, the Torah, the Prophets clarified. The Prophet Isaiah[10] reminds Israel that they were to engage the weekly Sabbath as an *oneg*, or delight and pleasure, a synonym with *eden*, as in The Garden of Eden. Shabbat was not something to be dreaded or endured until one could open his shop or fire up the oven again. It was an anticipation of resurrection and return to the Garden of Eden.

When Isaiah reminds Israel of this delightful relationship to the Sabbath, he assumes they already understand that the Sabbath is a love relationship, not a forced break in the week. Some traditional thinking must have emerged from the written commandment to draw out the spirit of the Sabbath, not just the letter. In a similar concern for preserving the spirit of the Sabbath commandment(s), the Pharisees developed practical applications.

10. 68:13

14

If Shabbat is for Israelites to enjoy thanksgiving meals of what they have "boiled" and "baked," then how could they keep the cooked food warm to maximize the enjoyment, the oneg? The scholars examined acceptable ways for an already-kindled fire to hold the foods warm through the Shabbat. In some communities, shared common ovens were kindled before Shabbat, and they smoldered throughout the next day. Many families kept pots of food warm in them for the Sabbath meals. Foods that retained taste on low heat evolved, and today *cholents*, or stews, are used by Jews from many geographic regions. Each cholent recipe reflects the culture from which that family lived, such as Eastern Europe or the Middle East, and each recipe reflects the individual family's unique recipe.

In fact, in turn of the century Jerusalem, the common ovens held pots for communities of Jews. One example is the neighborhood of *Even Israel* in Nachlaot, which was built in 1875. While most Jewish neighborhoods were divided into Ashkenazi (European), Mizrachi (Middle Eastern), or Sephardic (Spanish or Near East), the *Even Israel* neighborhood was integrated. "The Story of the Stove"[11] is that when children were sent to retrieve the pots of cooked food for the Shabbat meals, sometimes they would mistake the cooking pots and return home with the wrong one. Suddenly, Moroccan Jews were eating European foods, Sephardic Jews were eating Mizrachi foods, and Europeans were consuming the spicy *charif*, exotic flavors of the Middle East and Mediterranean. Israeli cuisine today reflects these Shabbat "accidents" of culture.

This briefest of histories distills how the ancient instruction of the written Torah is now the essence of even a Jewish family recipe. The seed of the written Torah ultimately is grown (not added) into community and family customs.

11. Ulpan-Or, "Schunat Nachlaot," p. 9

Torah text as received by Moses

⬇

"Oral Law," or explanations as given to Moses[12]

⬇

Scholarly clarifications and practical application added to the Oral Law

⬇

Cultural applications

⬇

Family traditions

12. According to the tradition, these oral explanations were given by Moses to Joshua, from Joshua to the Elders, from the Elders to the Prophets, from the Prophets to the Men of the Great Assembly. (Avot 1:1) While this historical succession seems fantastic, the text itself refers to instructions or commandments given to Moses that are not included in the written text. (Dt 12:21)

The Torah was a living document for a living group of people. Its language, Hebrew, was not a dead, but a living language. Most Christian scholars studied the Torah as history or an abstraction from their own "living" New Testament, and the TANAKH (Old Testament) became more of a theoretical or eschatological study. The Jews, on the other hand, studied, spoke, read, and lived the verses of the Torah at the most basic level of life. It was more than theology, it affected daily life and culture.

One of human psychology's essential truths is summarized in Abraham Maslow's Hierarchy of Needs. Maslow's five-tier hierarchy of needs is a pyramid structure:

> Maslow stated that people are motivated to achieve certain needs and that some needs take precedence over others. *Our most basic need is for physical survival,* and this will be the first thing that motivates our behaviour. Once that level is fulfilled, the next level up is what motivates us, and so on.
>
> This five stage model can be divided into deficiency needs and growth needs. The first four levels are often referred to as deficiency needs, and the top level is known as growth or being needs.
>
> The deficiency needs are said to motivate people when they are unmet. Also, the need to fulfil such needs will become stronger the longer the duration they are denied. For example, the longer a person goes without food, the more hungry (sic) they will become...Once these growth needs have been reasonably satisfied, one may be able to reach the highest level called self-actualization. (McCleod, 2007)

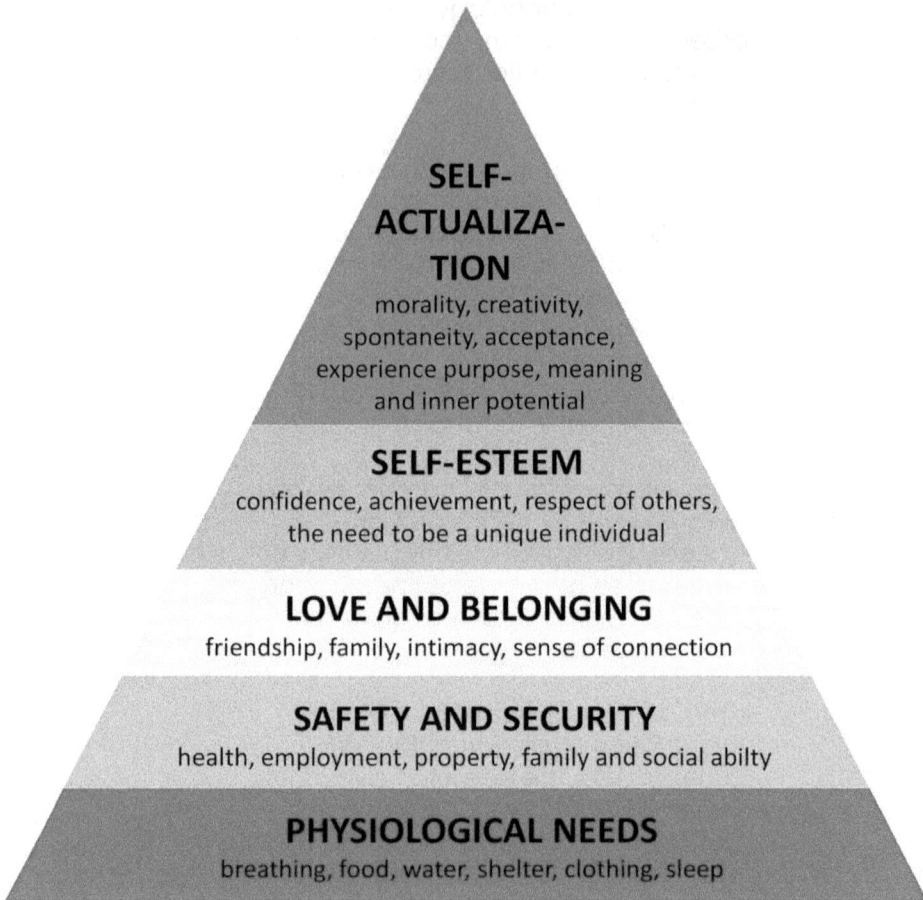

SELF-
ACTUALIZA-
TION
morality, creativity,
spontaneity, acceptance,
experience purpose, meaning
and inner potential

SELF-ESTEEM
confidence, achievement, respect of others,
the need to be a unique individual

LOVE AND BELONGING
friendship, family, intimacy, sense of connection

SAFETY AND SECURITY
health, employment, property, family and social abilty

PHYSIOLOGICAL NEEDS
breathing, food, water, shelter, clothing, sleep

Figure 1

The Apostle James alluded to this basic truth of being human when he wrote to "The twelve tribes scattered abroad" concerning the poor:

> If a brother or sister is without clothing and in need of daily food, and one of you says to them, 'Go in peace, be warmed and be filled,' and yet you do not give them what is

necessary for their body, what use is that? (Ja 2:15-16)

Professor Darrell L. Whiteman of Asbury Theological Seminary specializes in anthropology as it relates to spreading the message of Yeshua's mission. In a class lecture, he reminded his students that those who desire to take the salvation message to an ethnic group outside their own must understand that culture is a way of meeting this hierarchy of human needs.

For Jews, the Torah permeates every single level, not just higher-level needs for intellectual or spiritual growth. For the observant Jew, the most basic needs of fire and food are regulated by the Torah. This is the foundation of life that will lead to the higher levels of spiritual fulfillment. Culture manifests itself in how one relates to family, friends, neighbors, religion, food, education, and work, everything on the pyramid. For a Jew who is defined by the Torah, then Torah will manifest in how he relates culturally in every aspect of his life, for culture is part of addressing those needs.

For this reason, keeping Torah commandments is considered "Jewish" by the non-Jewish world even though they naturally keep many of the same commandments, such as not stealing, honoring one's parents, appointing courts and judges, or abhorring incest. Non-Jews may also have a cultural way of keeping those commandments, or it may be more individual. Because the Torah is inextricably tied to every part of Jewish culture, this can lead to a number of stereotypes about Jews and Judaism. For observant Jews, Torah is something lived within like-minded communities; the life of the individual within the community is linked tightly to the whole.

Think about how just observing the dietary laws of the Torah would limit pioneering. If I am not permitted to eat squirrels, lizards, rabbits, or other unclean animals, then how far or fast will I explore if I depend upon the community as a source of food? Human exploration and colonization was conducted by human beings willing to put anything into their mouths that did not immediately poison them. These explorers were therefore free to live months or years outside of a spiritual and cultural community.

The Word of God is designed to be lived in a community of faith. Personal religious freedom is at the same time a blessing and a frustration. For Torah-observant Jews, maintaining community is primary, and every other consideration is secondary. A community of faith is the foundation on which the Jewish family is built, lived, and perpetuated to guard the precepts of the Torah.

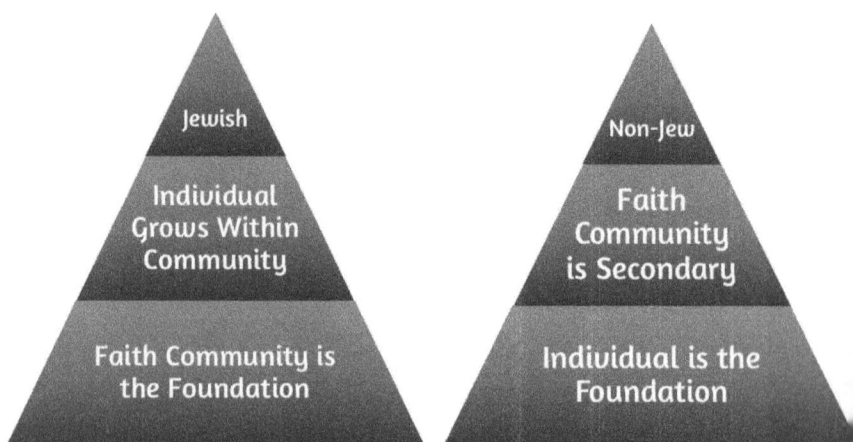

Jewish

Individual Grows Within Community

Faith Community is the Foundation

Non-Jew

Faith Community is Secondary

Individual is the Foundation

Whereas most American Christian denominations[13] exercise great religious freedom, the contrast in culture is acute. One people's concern is personal religious *independence* to worship, while the other's is community *dependence* for worship. In fact, one of the worst punishments imposed on the Israelite covenant community is *karet*, or being cut off from the community. Most Christians today apply the word "cult" to a religious community that is tightly-knit whether it meets the actual criteria for a cult or not.

13. There are exceptions, such as Amish or Mennonite communities.

The Apostle James, half-brother of Yeshua, wrote another caution in his letter to the "Twelve Tribes Scattered Abroad":

> Let not many of you become teachers, my brethren, knowing that as such we will incur a stricter judgment. (Ja 3:1)

This warning to believers in Yeshua is profound, for it explains many passages of the Gospels in which Yeshua reprimands either "Jews"[14] or "scribes and Pharisees." Corrections begin with those in leadership who need correction, and it is to the worst examples of these groups that Yeshua addresses his strongest corrections. The teacher judgment (G2917: *krima*) of which James speaks is often used in this context:

> condemnation of wrong, the decision (whether severe or mild) which one passes on the faults of others

The Pharisees and the scribes were teachers who guided their communities of First Century Jews. The average Jew, like most people, did not have enough time or wealth to engage in full-time Torah study. When their motivations and actions were inconsistent with both the letter *and* the spirit of the Torah, the Pharisees were behaving inconsistently *with their own schools.* Yeshua was obligated to point this out, and, as James wrote, to condemn it as any other sincere rabbi or Pharisee of the First Century would have done. Rabbis who didn't speak up in the presence of a wrong led to the destruction of the Second Temple, an event detailed in a later chapter. Those who don't practice what they preach do enter into greater condemnation.

The spiritual, and therefore, ethical, standards for the community were set by priests, scribes, and scholars such as the Pharisees. For Yeshua to point

14. There are scholarly sources that explain the First Century cultural, religious, political, and even ethnic "Judean" contrasted with a Galilean Jew. Considering the wide differences, the English translations of "the Jews" can be so imprecise as to leave the reader painting "the Jews" with the character of the worst examples. This point will be explained in the chapter entitled "The Judeans and the Heavy Yoke."

out hypocrisies within his own ethnic and religious community was both expected and practiced by other rabbis. The doctrinal and ethical divides of the First Century are as critical to decoding the Gospel texts as it is for a Muslim to understand the differences between Sunni and Shia or an Irishman the divide between Protestant and Catholic.

Not discerning intra-faith differences can cause one to blunder into hostile literal or conversational territory. Likewise, not discerning the differences among First Century Jews and Pharisees can lead Gospel readers to dangerous conclusions. To know the differences can clarify some of Yeshua's teachings, such as the command to listen to the scribes and Pharisees who sit in Moses' seat, yet not to do what they do! If someone is teaching the Word, obey him or her, but if they teach it and do something different, then *don't* do what they do. Adonai will judge them more harshly if they don't practice what they preach, so use the Word they teach as a guideline.

To help the student of Scripture read intelligently from the source, this booklet offers concise definitions of the "Judaisms" of the First Century. Sometimes a brief, accurate comparison and contrast of the groups is sufficient to unlock the dynamics of key passages within the texts.

Along with explanations of each group's identity is a characterization of each group based on its core doctrinal beliefs. These beliefs, such as the resurrection of the dead or validity of the Oral Law,[15] are vital to putting a face to the Gospel speakers. The goal is not to romanticize or demonize the Pharisees. The goal is to present historical facts so that the student can analyze every reference to the Pharisees, applying fair weights and measures that the Word adjures. Dr. Jimmilea Berryhill writes insightfully about the cultural influence on theology:

15. Strong's G#3862 *paradosis*

22

> Until recently, scholarship gave little consideration to the culture of the time in which biblical instructions were delivered. Seldom did research questions include those involving conflicting Scriptures or even how the passages might have been dealing primarily with a cultural norm that would not apply today. However, we must be careful not to dilute Scripture to a cultural acclamation. Accurately studied, culture will not in any way nullify a principle or law of God. (1999, p. 23)

The reader will find that the Pharisees are like the groups within any faith. There are good, bad, indifferent, righteous, hypocritical, and everything on the scale in between. In fact, their own writings record the good traits and praise them; they also record the problems, such as hypocrisy, and condemn them.

# 2

## STEREOTYPES: BEATEN BEFORE THE START

Ask your friends, "What is a Pharisee?" The likely answers are:

- Hypocrite
- Greedy
- Proud
- Self-righteous
- Mean

Hopefully the word "Jews" won't be on the list, but it is possible. Those stereotypes are not seen as stereotypes by those who use them. The Scriptures, after all, supply their proof texts. If a text is misunderstood, however, the Pharisees are beaten before they ever start to make an accurate impression on the reader. Much of the richness of the dialogues with them is lost.

Before examining some of those proof texts, it is

wise to define a stereotype to ensure that one has not fallen into that trap. It is very easy to mistake a proof text for a stereotype when the interpretation is unchallenged.

A stereotype is:

> A standardized mental picture that is held in common by members of a group and that represents an oversimplified opinion, prejudiced attitude, or uncritical judgment.

By "uncritical judgment," the definition means that the mental picture is not subjected to logical, analytical standards of judgment. Stereotyping can go hand-in-hand with ethnocentricism, which is:

> The attitude that one's own group, ethnicity, or nationality is superior to others.

Most Bible students have a basic understanding of Bible reference sources, how the Biblical canon was decided, and who wrote or recorded its books and letters. If the reference source is biased, however, it can affect one's definition or perception of a group of people from the outset. It is difficult to correct a distorted first perception. For instance, here is a Bible dictionary definition of a Pharisee that is available from a popular Bible software[16] application:

> Pharisee - a member of an ancient Jewish sect, distinguished by strict observance of the traditional and written law, and **commonly held to have pretensions to superior sanctity a self-righteous person; a hypocrite.** Old English *fariseus*, via ecclesiastical Latin from Greek *Pharisaios*, from Aramaic prīšayyā 'separated ones' (related to Hebrew pārūsh

16. LOGOS

26

'separated').

Nicely embedded among the scholarly description is a departure into stereotypes of how Pharisees came to be perceived in successive generations of Christian anti-Semitic polemics. Most people using a Bible dictionary already know what a Pharisee means today. Students of the Bible use a reference source, however, to find out what the word meant in its original use and context. If I am a new Bible student, then forever my first impression is that a Pharisee is and always was "commonly held to have pretensions to superior sanctity a self-righteous person; a hypocrite."

The logical conclusion for a student using the reference book is that "Pharisees are hypocrites." Although dictionaries are usually credible sources, the Bible student is not served well with this entry. Perhaps another reliable source, such as Strong's, will do better. Strong's[17] definition of a Pharisee is even more damning:

> A sect that started after the Jewish exile. In addition to OT books the Pharisees recognised in oral tradition a standard of belief and life. They sought for distinction and praise by **outward observance of external rites and by outward forms of piety, and such as ceremonial washings, fastings, prayers, and alms giving; and, comparatively negligent of genuine piety, they prided themselves on their fancied good works.** They held strenuously to a belief in the existence of good and evil angels, and to the expectation of a Messiah; and they cherished the hope that the dead, after a preliminary experience either of reward or of penalty in Hades, would

17. Retrieved 9/3/18 from *https://www. blueletterbible. org/ lang/ lexicon/ lexicon.cfm? Strongs=G5330 &t=NKJV*

27

be recalled to life by him, and be requited each according to his individual deeds. In opposition to the usurped dominion of the Herods and the rule of the Romans, they stoutly upheld the theocracy and their country's cause, and possessed great influence with the common people. **They were bitter enemies of Jesus and his cause; and were in turn severely rebuked by him for their avarice, ambition, hollow reliance on outward works, and affection of piety in order to gain popularity.**

This dictionary says that Pharisees were arch-enemies of Jesus, full of pride, greedy, prioritizing rituals over spiritual change, and popularity-seekers! It's not looking good for the Pharisees, but neither is it looking good for the new Bible student who will miss vital lessons that the Gospels, Acts, and even Revelation teach about the Pharisees. In fact, almost obscured by the stereotypical characteristics is the accurate information the student truly needs:

They held strenuously to a belief in the existence of good and evil angels, and to the expectation of a Messiah; and they cherished the hope that the dead, after a preliminary experience either of reward or of penalty in Hades, would be recalled to life by him [resurrection], and be requited each according to his individual deeds.

Presented with two kinds of information about the Pharisees, that which is analytical and that which is filtered through stereotype, many unsuspecting readers will adopt the stereotype; after all, it does make for juicy reading! The problem with both dictionaries, though, is the omitted defining texts about the Pharisees from *all* the contexts, both written and historical. The Bible records some wonderful things about individual Pharisees, and the very coming of Messiah was to a stage prepared by the Pharisees' fundamental doctrines.

These dictionaries' definitions encase the real meat of Pharisaic faith between two large pieces of stereotypical bread, forcing the naïve reader into a dilemma. Either she must picture the Pharisees as greedy, ritualistic, proud haters of Jesus, or conclude that Pharisees preached the coming of Messiah and the resurrection of the dead. The fact that both dictionaries' definitions include the modern pejorative use of Pharisee is troubling, for the writers of the definitions have succumbed to ethnocentric stereotypes unwittingly or purposely.

The problem goes beyond stereotypes. The definitions lure the reader into a logical fallacy, which is a form of mind manipulation. This particular fallacy is commonly called The Hasty Generalization. A Hasty Generalization draws a general rule from atypical cases.

> Example:
>
> (1) My Christian neighbor tells off-color jokes.
>
> Therefore:
>
> (2) Christians tell off-color jokes.

This argument takes an individual case of a Christian and draws a general rule from it, assuming that all Christians are like the atypical neighbor. The conclusion is foolish because it doesn't demonstrate a common characteristic of all Christians. It may be that the neighbor is not a typical Christian, so the conclusion is false. Maybe he goes to church because it's a way of establishing business contacts.

The truth is that many more neighbors may come forward who have never heard their Christian neighbors tell off-color jokes.

Why would Bible readers fall for stereotypes and the most obvious of logical fallacies? Probably because they want to believe them. This does not mean the reader is evil, racist, or anti-Semitic! It means the reader was never given the study tools to come to a different conclusion. The truly motivated reader may do the work to check out the better examples of Pharisaic behavior and research Jewish history for a less biased understanding, but many won't.

There are many psychological processes at work. Human beings need a David-and-Goliath story, a feel-good drama in which the bad guys are conquered by the good guy in spite of overwhelming odds, and in the end, the bad guys get their come-uppance. Good conquers evil. Truth conquers tradition. Our fascination with superheroes is not religious, but the premise is the same. No one seems to care that superhero stories require a villain who is completely evil without any redeeming qualities, and those are rare in real life. This is necessary to the story; otherwise, the reader might question why the superhero so often chooses total annihilation of his foe.

Human beings are also a bit lazy. They want the greatest return with the least amount of effort. If Bible teachers conclude that the Pharisees were all greedy hypocrites, and at first glance, the Gospels appear to agree with that conclusion, then there's no reason to waste time researching it. The valued knowledge is achieved with little effort, but what if the valuable "truth" is inaccurate?

Finally, and sadly, some readers are insecure in their faith or even their own personal worth. It feels good when the Bible can be used to prove that we are superior to other people groups, especially the one that the Bible says is His Chosen People. We're special after all, and no matter what our grace-covered, trivial transgressions, at least we're not one of those despicable Pharisees or Jews who tormented our Lord and Savior Jesus Christ!

The Bible text itself will be the best teacher and definer of a Pharisee, and the Pharisees' own analysis of their sect can help the Bible student form a more accurate definition of the Pharisees. It is important to have a good definition of a Pharisee, for they played a fundamental role in First Century Messianic expectation and the spread of the gospel.

What many students do not know are basic historical facts that affect one's reading of the text, especially in a translation such as English. For instance, the *New American Standard Bible* reads thus:

> No servant can serve two masters; for either he will hate the one and love the other, or else he will be devoted to one and despise the other. You cannot serve God and weath.
>
> Now the Pharisees, who were lovers of money, were listening to all these things and were scoffing at Him.
>
> And He said to them, 'You are those who justify yourselves in the sight of men, but God knows your hearts; for that which is highly esteemed among men is detestable in the sight of God.' (Lk 16:13-15)

The appositive phrase, "who were lovers of money," is enclosed with commas. The English translator's grammar doesn't just imply, but states, that *all* the Pharisees were lovers of money. Is this the best place for commas?

New Testament Greek, like the Hebrew of the TANAKH, was not written with punctuation or capital letters. For instance, here is an example of a TANAKH Hebrew text:

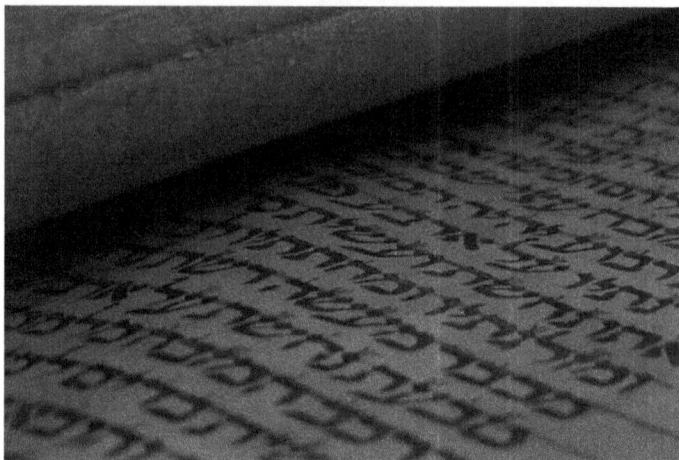

Figure 3

No punctuation or capital letters there! The New Testament letters were usually delivered by people who knew the writer's intent and explained or taught it, such as Phoebe for Paul's letter to the Romans. It ensured that the lack of punctuation did not result in misunderstanding. Here is an example of Greek text:

CΚΑΙCΙΛΘΝΔΙΟΤΙΕΕΝΓΗCΕΔΡΑΧ'ΚΑΙΔ
ΛΗΜΜΑΛΟΓΟΥ᠎᠎ΙCΚΑΙCΙΛΘΝΔΙΟΤΙΕ
ΕΝΓΗCΕΔΡΑΧ'ΚΑΙΔΦΡΟΡΗCΑCΦΟΔΡΑ'
ΑΜΑCΚΟΥΘΥCΙΑΛΥΚΑΙΩΚΟΛΟΜΗCΕΝ
ΤΟΥ᠎ΤΙΚCΕΦΡΑΤΥΡΟCΟΧΥΡΩΜΑ
ΑΝΘΡΩΠΟΥCΚΠΑCΤΑΛΥΤΗC'ΚΑΙΕΘΗ
ΑCΦΥΛΑCΤΟΥΙΗΧ'CΑΥΡΙCΕΝΑΡΓΥΡΕ
ΚΑΙΕΝΕΜΑΘ'ΕΤΟΙCΙΟΝΩCΧΟΥΚΑΙΧΡΥ
ΟΡΙΟΙCΑΥΤΗC'ΤΥΡΟΛΗΜΜΑΛΟΓΟΥ᠎
CΚΑΙCΙΔΘΝΔΙΟΤΙΕΕΝΓΗCΕΔΡΑΧ'ΚΑΙΔ
ΦΡΟΡΗCΑCΦΟΔΡΑ'ΑΜΑCΚΟΥΘΥCΙΑΛΥ
ΚΑΙΩΚΟΛΟΜΗCΕΝΤΟΥ᠎ΤΙΚCΕΦΡΑ
ΤΥΡΟCΟΧΥΡΩΜΑΑΝΘΡΩΠΟΥCΚΠΑC
ΤΑΛΥΤΗC'ΚΑΙΕΘΗΑCΦΥΛΑCΤΟΥΙΗΧ
CΑΥΡΙCΕΝΑΡΓΥΡΕΚΑΙΕΝΕΜΑΘ'ΕΤΟΙC
ΙΟΝΩCΧΟΥΚΑΙΧΡΥΟΡΙΟΙCΑΥΤΗC'ΤΥΡΟ
ΛΗΜΜΑΛΟΓΟΥ᠎CΚΑΙCΙΔΘΝΔΙΟΤΙΕ
ΕΝΓΗCΕΔΡΑΧ'ΚΑΙΔΦΡΟΡΗCΑCΦΟΔΡΑ'
ΑΜΑCΚΟΥΘΥCΙΑΛΥΚΑΙΩΚΟΛΟΜΗCΕΝ
ΤΟΥ᠎ΤΙΚCΕΦΡΑΤΥΡΟCΟΧΥΡΩΜΑ
ΑΝΘΡΩΠΟΥCΚΠΑCΤΑΛΥΤΗC'ΚΑΙΕΘΗ
ΑCΦΥΛΑCΤΟΥΙΗΧ'CΑΥΡΙCΕΝΑΡΓΥΡΕ
ΚΑΙΕΝΕΜΑΘ'ΕΤΟΙCΙΟΝΩCΧΟΥΚΑΙΧΡΥ
ΟΡΙΟΙCΑΥΤΗC'ΤΥΡΟΛΗΜΜΑΛΟΓΟΥ᠎

Figure 4

Again, there is no punctuation. What if the sentence is re-written without the translator's commas?

> Now the Pharisees who were lovers of money were listening to all these things and were scoffing at Him.

With this punctuation, the reader is not tempted to paint all Pharisees as money-lovers with a broad brush. Among those Pharisees who were listening, those who *did* love money began to scoff at him. In any church, there is a usually a subgroup who may attend faithfully, yet they are there only for business contacts or to be seen "doing the right thing" in order to maintain community standing. Why would we expect Pharisees to be different than any other religious denomination?

Perhaps the better question is what Pharisees

*themselves* thought of hypocrites or the greedy among their own sect.  The *Mishnah* is the code of Jewish Oral Law that was written down after the destruction of the Second Temple. Unlike the *Talmud*, which expanded until the Middle Ages, the *Mishnah* most closely represents the history, culture, and thought patterns of First Century Jews.  In its most ethical of sections, called the *Pirkei Avot*,[18] it is possible to read exactly what the Pharisees handed down to the Jews of the early rabbinic period following the second destruction of the Temple.

*Pirkei Avot* tells today's reader what the "normal" Pharisee thought about greed, generosity, and money.

- On three things the world stands: on the Torah, on the service [prayer] and on acts of lovingkindness. [charity] (Avot 1:2)
- Do not be as servants who are serving the master in order to receive a reward, rather be as servants who are serving the master not in order to receive a reward; and may the fear of Heaven be upon you." (Avot 1:3)
- May your home be open wide, may the poor be members of your household. (Avot 1:5)
- The more flesh, the more worms. The more possessions, the more worry... The more charity, the more peace.  (Avot 2:7)
- The evil eye [stinginess], the evil inclination, and hatred of the creations remove a person from the world. (Avot 2:11)
- Who is rich? The one who is satisfied with what he has...(Avot 4:1)
- The money of your friend should be as dear to you as your own. (Avot 2:12)
- Minimize business and engage in Torah. Be humble of spirit before everyone. (Avot 4:10)
- [The one who says] "what is mine is yours, and what is yours is yours" -- [that's a] pious person. [One who says] "what is

yours is mine, and what is mine is mine"
-- [that's a] wicked person. (Avot 5:10)
- There are four temperaments among givers of charity: One who wishes to give, but [that] others not give -- he has an evil eye [stingy] with respect to others. [One who wishes that] others give, and he [himself] not give -- he has an evil eye [stingy] with respect to himself. [One who wishes to] give and [that] others give -- [that's a] pious person. [One who wishes] not to give and [that] others not give -- [that's a] wicked person. (Avot 5:13)

The Pharisees themselves rebuked the greedy among their own. Were there greedy Pharisees? Of course! This is why the problem was addressed by Pharisees. These flaws were not acceptable among Jews, a fact that Yeshua also preached. The Word is to transform Israel into generous people, not stingy ones.

Another stereotype is that all Pharisees were hypocrites, for the eight woes pronounced upon hypocritical Pharisees in the Gospel of Matthew has caused most readers to believe that all scribes and Pharisees were cursed hypocrites. Again, Yeshua is calling out those within the greater group, for just because one is zealous for the Law (Torah) does not mean he is a hypocrite:

> And when they heard it they began glorifying God; and they said to him, 'You see, brother, how many thousands there are among the Jews of those who have believed, and they are all zealous for the Law...' (Acts 21:20)

Here is what the Pharisees themselves said of those who were proud or hypocritical, and even the scoffers:

- Be very, very humble in spirit, for the hope of man is worms. (Avot 4:4)
- Do not disparage anyone, and do not shun any thing. For you have no man who does not have his hour, and you have no thing that does not have its place. (Avot 4:3)
- One who withholds himself from judging - removes from himself enmity, theft, and the false oath. One who is nonchalant about giving legal decisions is an imbecile, wicked, and arrogant in spirit. (Avot 4:7)
- Do not make the Torah into a crown with which to aggrandize yourself, and not into a spade with which to dig into them. And thus Hillel used to say: And one who makes use of the crown [of learning] passes away. From here you learn that anyone who benefits [greedily] from the words of the Torah removes his life from the world. (Avot 4:5)
- Let the honor of your student be dear to you as your own, and the honor of your fellow like the reverence of your teacher, and the reverence of your teacher like the reverence of Heaven. (Avot 4:12)
- Envy, lust and [coveting] honor drive a man from the world. (Avot 4:21)
- Blessed be He, who has before Him no wrong, no forgetfulness, no respect of persons, no taking of bribes, for all is His. (Avot 4:22)
- Do not seek greatness for yourself, and do not covet honor. More than your study, do. And do not desire the tables of kings since your table is greater than their tables and your crown is greater than their crowns. (Avot 6:5)
- Anyone who has these three things is from the students of Abraham, our father, and [anyone who has] three other things is from the students of Balaam the evildoer: [one who has] a good eye [generous], a humble spirit and a small appetite -- is from the

students of Abraham, our father. [One who has] an evil eye [stingy], a haughty spirit and a broad appetite - is from the students of Balaam the evildoer. But the students of Balaam the evildoer inherit Gehinnom and go down to the pit of destruction, as it is stated (Psalms 55:24), 'And You, God, will bring them down to the pit of destruction; the people of blood and deceit, they will not live out half their days; and I will trust in You.' ...classes of people that do not receive the Divine Presence (Sotah 42a). A company of scoffers, as it is written, 'He stretches out his hand with scorners' (Hos. 7:8). A company of liars, as it is written, 'He that speaks falsehood shall not be established before mine eyes' (Ps. 101:7). A company of flatterers, as it is written, 'That a hypocrite cannot come before Him' (Job 13:16). (quoted in Orchot Tzaddikim)

It is apparent from other texts that normative Pharisaism despised hypocrisy among its own. Take this passage in Matthew Twenty-three as an example. In the NASB version of the Bible, translators added this subtitle:

**Pharisaism Exposed**

Yes, the Pharisees were beaten even before the English translator translated one word of the chapter.

> Then Jesus spoke to the crowds and to His disciples, saying: 'The scribes and the Pharisees have seated themselves in the chair of Moses; therefore, all that they tell you, do and observe, but do not do according to their deeds; for they say things and do not do them.' (Mt 23:1-3)

Sincere Pharisees also despised those who were teaching the Word, yet not abiding by it themselves. Klausner comments that "The last words can be applied to the best of religious bodies and to the best of people." We all say one thing and do another at times. This neither characterizes our whole lives, nor the lives of people with whom we worship or share our faith. Klausner continues with documentation from the Talmud, which condemns those "who require what is good but do not practice it."[19]

In amusing irony, the Jewish tradition goes beyond Yeshua's warning about hypocrites. Yeshua politely calls them "Pharisees." The rabbis name names:

> Seemly are the words when they
> come from the mouth of them
> which practice them; some there
> be which require what is good and
> also practice it: Ben Azzai requires
> what is good, but does not practice
> it. (Klausner, p. 366, quoting from
> Yevamot VIII 4)

Ben Azzai was put on notice...in print...for his hypocrisy. It's a good thing they don't do that in church bulletins!

Related to hypocrisy is false piety. This is how the rabbis received it from the proto-rabbis of the Pharisees:

> ...those who stumbled into walls in
> the zealousness to avoid looking at
> a woman in the street; the Shechem
> Pharisee, whose dishonesty and
> ostentation was like that of the
> people of Shechem; the Pharisee
> who was always stumbling over his
> own feet because he was trying
> to walk humbly; the Pharisee who
> was always inquiring of others what

19. p. 366, quoted from Chagigah 14a and Yevamot 63b

38

the proper ritual was, not because
he really wanted to know, but only
so that he could show off that he
had already fulfilled everything; the
Pharisee who acted only for the sake
of the rewards he would receive
in the world to come; and the
Pharisee who acted only out of fear
of punishment in the world to come.
(from Sotah 22b, paraphrased in
Dalman, 2002, p. 44)

The Pharisees believed in giving dignity even to the poor, not just the wealthy. Those who coveted the best seats in the synagogues or at banquets were acknowledged to be spiritually deficient, not the ideal. According to the Pharisees, scoffers such as those who scoffed at Yeshua, are among those who "do not receive the Divine Presence." The normal Pharisee despised false piety.

While most Bible students would not automatically categorize a rich person as evil, it would be easy to use the same stereotype as is used with the Pharisees. There are a few instances in Scripture where it speaks of the rich as evil, such as:

Is it not the rich who oppress you and
personally drag you into court? Do
they not blaspheme the fair name
by which you have been called? (Ja
2:6-7)

If we take out of context this or Yeshua's caution about it being difficult for a rich man to enter the Kingdom of Heaven, then it may appear that *all* rich men are evil blasphemers who oppress poor people. The full context of Scripture, however, has examples of generous righteous rich men and women, such as Job, Abraham, the Queen of Sheba, Lydia, Joseph of Arimathea, or the high-ranking[20] Pharisee[21] Nicodemus, who did not consent to Yeshua's death[22] in the "kangaroo court" assembled by the Sadducees:

> When it was evening, there came a rich man from Arimathea, named Joseph, who himself had also become a disciple of Jesus. This man went to Pilate and asked for the body of Jesus. Then Pilate ordered it to be given to him. And Joseph took the body and wrapped it in a clean linen cloth, and laid it in his own new tomb... (Mt 27:57-60)

> Nicodemus, who had first come to Him by night, also came, bringing a mixture of myrrh and aloes, about a hundred pounds weight. (Jn 19:39)

Stereotyping certainly removes a lot of the burden to diligently study the Scriptures, but taking full context is a challenge and hard work. It requires putting together not just the simple meaning of the text, but what it meant to the people who spoke the words. To the Pharisee of the First Century, a truly and spiritually rich person was "the one who is satisfied with what he has..." (Avot 4:1)

Alternatively, another type of rich person was spiritually deficient, greedy, and had a grander view of himself than any honorable Pharisee should have. This type of rich person is not just found lurking among the First Century Pharisees; he is lurking among the end-time Seven Assemblies of Revelation:

20. Mk 15:43

21. Jn 3:1

22. Lk 23:51

> So because you are lukewarm, and neither hot nor cold, I will spit you out of My mouth. Because you say, 'I am rich, and have become wealthy, and have need of nothing,' and you do not know that you are wretched and miserable and poor and blind

and naked... (Re 3:16-17)

The language in Revelation is reminiscent of the quotation from *Pirkei Avot*. The spiritually rich person is satisfied with the earthly goods that he has. This makes him truly "have need of nothing," for he trusts Adonai to meet his needs. The obverse is true. Those who are satisfied that they are already sufficient in spiritual goods will find that they are very poor, and in fact, they need much more to be rich in the Kingdom! Like Yeshua said, they look good on the outside with acts of piety, but the inside is a grave of the spirit.

The true, "hot" rich man will be content with his earthly goods, but he will never cease seeking greater spiritual riches. A lukewarm man will never be content with his earthly goods, so he will neglect his search for greater spiritual riches. One cannot serve God and money, so money enslaves the lukewarm man who thought he was independently wealthy.

Another example of English word selection is in the following verse:

> And when he was **demanded** [*eperotao*] **of the Pharisees**, when the kingdom of God should come, he answered them and said, 'The kingdom of God cometh not with observation...' (Lk 17:20 KJV)

The Greek word (G1905) *eperotao* is translated as "demand." The verb is from G1909 and G2065, which mean:

> to ask for, i.e. inquire, seek: ask (after, questions), demand, desire, question.

The translation of "demanded" is most puzzling, for how many times is that particular Greek word translated as the more innocuous "asked" instead of the emotionally-charged "demanded"? For English-speakers, there is a marked visceral difference in the reaction to someone who asks or inquires versus someone who demands.

The KJV translates Strong's G1905 with the following English words:

> ask (53x)
> demand (2x)
> desire (1x)
> ask question (1x)
> question (1x)
> ask after (1x)

Although the translators select "ask" 53 times in other contexts, in relation to the Pharisees, they select "demand," one of only two times the word is translated with such negativity! This does not mean that the English Bible is chock-full of poor word selections. It means that study tools are freely available when a reader sees that something just doesn't add up.

Stereotyping the Pharisees is an unfortunate inheritance that has contributed to persecutions and murders of Jews around the world. Bible scholars note that Christian stereotyping of the Jews was not founded on critical, analytical judgment that weighs all contexts, including historical context:

> ...[Gospel] history has been the subject of stereotyping and rhetorical flourish rather than the subject of close and critical investigation. (Azar, 2016)

> As historical critics of this period foregrounded the recognitions that the gospel's authors were Jewish, that Jesus was Jewish, that

the earliest followers were Jewish,
and that the whole portrayal was
essentially an inner-Jewish debate,
they were able to throw scholarly
weight against previous assertions
(especially under the Third Reich)
that the gospel was somehow the
account of "Jesus/John against
Judaism," "Christianity against
Judaism," or, perhaps worst of all,
"Gentiles against Jews." Furthermore,
in emphasizing that the harsh
rhetoric contained within the Fourth
Gospel was not only a product of
an inner-Jewish debate but of a
*normal* inner-Jewish debate (by first-
century standards), commentators
established that John's Gospel was
actually fairly harmless in its historical
context—whatever the later effect
of its unfortunate rhetoric. (ibid)

The conversations that Yeshua had with Pharisees
and other Jews were part of *normal* religious
debate. One would not take the transcript of a
church meeting, highlight the beliefs of the worst
participants, and proclaim that they represent the
beliefs of the entire church. "No," many of those
present would say. "We were there to rebuke and
oppose them, not to agree with them!"

Likewise, the "Jews," which denoted the more
ritually-scrupulous, or in some cases, fanatical,
religious Jews of the south, were in contrast to the
more Roman-friendly (and a bit independent)
Galileans, who were less scrupulous in their religious
observance. While Peter waited on the outcome
of Yeshua's arrest, he was quickly identified as a
Galilean. He wasn't playing a banjo, but he stood
out nonetheless. Jews were as diverse as Americans
today, for the mainstream political and religious
beliefs of Manhattan are markedly different from

rural Alabama's.

While John's portrayal of "the Jews" may have led Gentile readers to believe that all Jews of all time were responsible for Jesus's death, one ancient Christian scholar, Cyril of Alexandria, objected:

> Though Cyril, like Chrysostom, was a well-known opponent of Judaism, he asserts that Jews as a whole cannot be blamed for the crucifixion of Jesus. As he *explicitly* says (commenting on John 19:5–6), "[It] is to the *leaders* of the Jews alone, it seems, that the wise Evangelist ascribed the origin of such impiety" (*Comm. Jo.* 12). (Azar, 2016)

Throughout history, ethnocentricity and stereotyping have characterized lazy scholarship and self-serving religion. Cyril may have been a reluctant anomaly to his contemporaries, but he nevertheless applied critical judgment to the text in spite of his opposition to Judaism. This grudging admission is verified by Yeshua's own words when he tells his disciples that he will be turned over to the chief priests who will condemn him to death. The problem is that the Jewish religious court could not execute the death penalty.

As Yeshua predicted, he was turned by the chief priests to the Gentiles, who did have the authority to execute him, which they did. (Mk 10:33-34; Mt 20:18-19; Lk 18:32-33). The most important lesson is that *all humankind* is responsible for the death of Yeshua, and therefore, all mankind can be saved through faith in his resurrection. If we do not admit our share in putting him to death, then we have no share in his eternal life.

The modern Biblical student can learn from Cyril's example that "right" and "wrong" or "good" and "evil" are oversimplifications, false dilemmas forced into the text. One must look at the whole context of the passage as well as many other passages with the same keywords or themes. The critical eye is important, for the lazy eye can lead one to call good evil or evil good.

Another example of a persisting stereotype has to do with good works and salvation. Imagine if we were to have a trial and actually call a Jew and his stereotyper to testify and offer evidence. The charge is one that has likely been repeated in many churches.

> The Stereotyper: "Jews are so confused. They think you can earn your salvation or righteousness by doing works of the Torah (Law). They are all about the letter of the law."

Imagine an impartial judge also calls an Orthodox Jew to the stand. The Jew carries a common *siddur*, a compilation of daily or festival prayers. Since all observant Jews pray them, such a book would be hard evidence. The Jew begins reading from the prayerbook:

> "I rely not on my deeds, but Your mercy..." (Selichos, p 308)

> "I have no deeds to my credit, no merit is in my hand." (p. 301)

> "Upon Your mercy do we trust..." (p. 297)

> "O God, for my sake go beyond the line [letter] of Your Law..." (p. 307)

> "Yours is the righteousness, and ours are the iniquities." (p. 295)

> "Not because of our righteousness
> do we cast down our supplications
> before You, rather because of Your
> abundant compassion." (p. 305)

> "Righteousness, which is Yours alone,
> is what we request..." (Selichos, p.
> 309)

The ancient Jewish prayers fly in the face of The Stereotyper's testimony. Perhaps The Stereotyper has confused *salvation* with *sanctification*. The Jewish prayerbook reader says,

> "Sanctify us in your
> commandments..."[23]

The Jew understands that commandments, or the "law," are for sanctification of a "saved" people. There are two garments for the individual, a garment of salvation and a garment of righteousness.

> I will rejoice greatly in the LORD,
> My soul will exult in my God;
> For He has clothed me with
> *garments of salvation*,
> He has wrapped me with a *robe of
> righteousness*,
> As a bridegroom decks himself with
> a garland,
> And as a bride adorns herself with
> her jewels. (Is 61:10)

Both garments are desirable, for they are wedding preparations!

23. Weekday
*Shmoneh Esrei*,
conclusion.

# 3

## WHAT IS A PHARISEE?

Who built the house next door? Most of the time, the house next door has always been there, so the neighbors rarely contemplate when it was built, who built it, why they built it, or how it was built. It's just there. Always has been.

Believers in Yeshua the Messiah take the resurrection for granted, but who developed the doctrine of resurrection from the Torah and Prophets? After all, it's not that clear from the first five books of the Bible. Just because readers are told in the New Testament that Isaac was a type of Messiah doesn't mean that it would be clear to a reader who didn't have the New Testament. The doctrine of resurrection is the house next door that is taken for granted by most Christians. History documents that it was the Pharisees who gave formation to this "house next door" from the Biblical text.

Because the Pharisees are present in the four gospels, it is useful to define the historical group and its origin. Pharisees, too, are a house next door to the Bible student. World and Jewish history contributed to the emergence of groups such as the Pharisees. A simplified historical progression helps the reader to pinpoint the key events that set the stage for the

Gospels and other New Testament letters.

---

Jews return from exile in Babylon
▼

Greeks come to power under Alexander the Great
▼

Alexander's death brings the division of his kingdom into four Greek empires; Judea comes under the control of the Seleucid Empire
▼

The Greek successors battle for control, affecting Judea because of its location
▼

Civil unrest arises in Judea between Hellenist Jews and those committed to the Torah as law
▼

At the instigation of many of the Hellenist Jews, the Greeks oppress the traditionalist Jews; they forbid circumcision, reading of the Torah; Greeks desecrate the Temple with pagan foods and idols
▼

The Hasmoneans (Maccabees) revolt against the Greeks and Hellenist Jews, prevailing after a protracted war
▼

Rome replaces the Greeks as a world power and puts Judea under Roman control

---

The period of Greek ascension to power birthed the early sects that emerged into a group known as the Pharisees. The Pharisees developed during the Maccabean Period from the "Hasidim" (pious ones). Several different groups like the Essenes came out of the anti-Hellenistic reaction to the Greek rulers over Judea, particularly Antiochus IV Epiphanes.

There were two main schools of thought that comprised the larger group called Pharisees: the House of Shammai and the House of Hillel. Briefly, this defines all Pharisees' major doctrines:

> A.  Belief in a coming Messiah.
> B.  God is active in daily life. This was directly opposite from the Sadducees.[24]
> C.  A physically-oriented afterlife based on earthly life, which involved reward and punishment.
> D.  Authority of the Old Testament and the Oral Traditions (Talmud).
> E.  Highly developed angelology. This involved both good and evil spiritual beings. (Utley, 2003, pp. 86-87)

The centuries between the Israelites' return from Babylon exile and the First Century are vital to understanding the multiple political, economic, religious, and military crises suffered by the Jews. For a brief history, see the author's *Seven Shepherds: Hanukkah in Prophecy*, or for a more thorough reading, the books of First and Second Maccabees are instructive. It was in this period of Greek and Roman world power that the Pharisees emerged in Jewish history.

Although Utley's description above is an academic Bible reference, there is an anachronistic error in "D." The Pharisees could not have believed in the *Talmud*, for its earliest pages were not written until two centuries after Messiah's death and resurrection. It was not finalized until the medieval period. The Pharisees were long gone from the history by then. Such errors, though they seem small, are common in Bible reference sources. The

24. Much of Pharisaic doctrine is a theological counterpoint to the Sadducees' doctrines.

Talmud represents a vast quantity, centuries' worth, of additional commentary and development from the Oral Traditions that existed during the time that the gospels were written.

### The Hasidim

With the few resources from the pre-gospel Biblical era or later documents alluding to that period, scholars have searched for how the Pharisaic movement arose:

> The Pharisaic movement arose in the 2nd century [BCE] with its many crises. Essentially more difficult to answer is the question to which circle Pharisaism owed its origin. (Kittel, p. 13)

Scholars guess that the Pharisees emerged as a sect known as Hasidim[25] prior to the Jewish Maccabean Revolt against Greece:

> The Chasidim appear for the first time at the beginning of the religious persecution under Antiochus IV Epiphanes (167/166 B.C.). According to 1 Macc. 2:42 the Maccabees, after a severe defeat, were joined by 'a company of Chasidim, brave men of Israel, each of whom gave himself willingly for the law. And all who fled before the disaster joined them and strengthened them and brought together a great army.' (ibid, p. 14)

25. Not to be confused with the modern Hasidic movement

Prior to the revolt, the Hasidim (*Chasidim* is a variant English spelling) resisted not the Greeks, but fellow Jews who had fallen into apostasy and assimilation with Greek culture. The Hasidim were independent of the ruling class of Hasmoneans, and it is possible that the Hasidim also formed the sect of Essenes: "the concept of Chasidim lives on indirectly in Aramaic form in the term Essene."[26] Textual evidence links the Hasidim, the Essenes, and the Essenes' stronghold in the Qumran, Matzad. Historically, the Essenes maintained a good relationship with the Pharisaic House of Hillel, so both the Essenes and the Pharisees may trace to the early group known as Hasidim.

To review, the Pharisees:

- Emerged from pious religious sects of Judaism that formed sometime in the last half of the 2nd Century BC.
- Believed in an afterlife, the "World to Come," resurrection of the body with the soul, and final judgment.
- Believed in an oral tradition that explained the written Torah.
- Believed in angels and a Messiah

In Hebrew, the Pharisees were called the *Prushim or Prushin*. The root word in Hebrew is *parash*:

> *Parash* פָּרַשׁ - to make distinct, declare, distinguish, separate (Qal) to declare, clarify (Pual) to be distinctly declared. To separate, literally (to disperse).

The definition of the word helps determine exactly what a Pharisee expected his religious affiliation and expression of his faith to accomplish. Scripture provides the context for *parash*:

> So they read in the book in the law of God distinctly (*parash*), and gave the sense, and caused *them* to understand the reading. (Ne 8:8)
>
> And they put him in custody, until the decision of the LORD should be

26. Kittel, Bromiley & Friedrich, p. 14.

made clear (*perosh*) to them. (Le 24:12 NRSV).

A *Parush* (Pharisee) was one who desired to give distinct sense to the Hebrew Biblical text and to disperse the knowledge so that the average person could understand it, and therefore, obey it.

For this reason, the Pharisees had the hearts of multitudes of common people, for they were a reformist sect, constantly seeking ethical improvement of the social, political, and religious systems. Because they were reformists, the Pharisees sometimes became involved in political intrigues, such as those with Herod or the Jewish Revolt, but many paid with their lives. This may have led to their later withdrawal to Yavneh on the eve of the Second Temple's destruction. They removed themselves from the political and military conflicts to simply focus on learning Scripture.

Unlike the earliest Hasidim, the later Pharisees generally were reformists who tried to work within a system rather than revolutionaries who wanted to overthrow foreign influence. For instance, it is believed that King Alexander Jannaeus (103–76 BCE) crucified 800 Pharisees as opponents,[27] but his successor, his wife Queen Alexandra, used the Pharisees to exert calm and control over the Judean people, and in return, she allowed them to influence her reign with religious law.

27. Saldarini, 2001, p. xvi

28. This is based on their sparse mention in Josephus' historical works, although he was also a Pharisee for a period.

The Pharisees were not as prevalent[28] as Bible readers would think, but one could expect they were over-represented as a group in the gospels because they were active in the sphere of religious activity. They would have been especially interested in another reformist who was preaching many of their doctrines and who was popular in the Galilee. Yeshua was of interest in the more religiously-fervent Judea, so it appears that sometimes Pharisees were dispatched to assess the Galilean preacher. Readers of the New Testament assume because of this that there were lots of Pharisees, but this was not so.

The Gospels highlight the Pharisees because their history was so connected doctrinally to Yeshua, and their paths frequently intersected, for they shared audiences. Since Yeshua's very life, death, and resurrection was a validation of the Pharisees' teaching, we might even say that the Pharisees prepared the stage for Yeshua's arrival in his particular generation. His preaching of resurrection fell on many Jewish ears prepared to hear. His Messianic works were believed by many Jewish eyes prepared to see.

In reality, though, the Pharisees were a small number of people. It was their doctrine of resurrection that brings them into Biblical focus, not their large numbers. "Because the Pharisees are prominent among Jewish groups mentioned in the New Testament, Biblical scholars tend to inflate their importance. From the viewpoint of the whole culture, and especially that of the ruling classes, the Pharisees were of minor importance."[29] The number of Pharisees at the time of Herod may have been around 6,000.[30] Various sources report that 3,000,000 – 4,000,000 Jews and converts filled Jerusalem during annual feasts, so the ratio of Pharisees to total population is very small.

The small number of Pharisees relative to the general population of First Century Jews tells the reader that their great impact both in the hearts of the common people and in the gospels was vital to the presentation of Yeshua's message.

29. Saldarini, 2001, p. 79

30. Saldarini, 2001, p. 99

# 4

## OTHER FIRST CENTURY JUDAISMS

There was no single "Judaism" of the First Century. Prior to the destruction of the Second Temple, there were many sects active in Judea and the Galilee. New Testament readers will be most familiar with Sadducees and Pharisees, but there were other sects such as the Ebionites and Essenes. Likewise, there were groups that were not sects of Judaism, but represented sacred occupations, such as the scribes or priests. These occupational or sectarian groups will orbit into the gospel accounts in some way, which can be a real puzzle to modern readers.

Hundreds of books have been written about these various groups, but a simple explanation will suffice in helping the reader grasp the simple dynamics of their gospel appearances. On the other hand, it will hint to the complexity of public and religious life in First Century Judea and Galilee.

## Sadducees

The Sadducees believed that only the laws of the Torah were authoritative, they rejected the resurrection of the dead as unprovable in the Torah, and they were influential among the rich. Since they did not believe in soul immortality, they denied rewards or punishments in judgment after death. They dominated the political priesthood in the First Century.

> The Pharisees in Jesus' day did not enjoy the dominant role in Palestinian Judaism which one might sometimes think from the Synoptic records. This means concretely that they did not yet play a normative part in the Sanhedrin at Jerusalem; in the days of Jesus, the Sadducees still exercised ultimate authority... according to the Synoptic tradition, the Pharisees no longer play any significant part in the story of the passion. This is obviously and indisputably an authentic and reliable reminiscence. (Kittel, Bromiley & Friedrich, 37)

The Jewish-Roman historian Josephus describes the Sadducees as "boorish and rude,"[31] even with one another. "Josephus notes that the Sadducees had the confidence of the rich, but he does not say that *all* the Sadducees were rich; much less does he say that *all* the rich, the rulers and the chief priests were Sadducees, a position often assumed by scholars."[32] Although this is frustrating when the reader wants a concrete depiction of *all* Sadducees, the truth is that what bound them together was their [lack of] belief of the afterlife, not economics.

Avoid the temptation to reduce historical people to good guys and bad guys or poor people and

31. Saldarini, 2001, p. 110

32. Saldarini, 2001, p. 117

rich people. Let each actor in the narrative speak for himself or herself, not the group. Since Acts documents that many of the "chief" religious leaders came to belief in Yeshua, one could surmise that even many of the Sadducees came to believe in the resurrection of the dead.

One reason the rich may have favored the Sadducees is their harsher judgment for crimes, which is in contrast with the Pharisees', which generally was more in line with our modern maxim of "innocent until proven guilty beyond a shadow of a doubt."

## Essenes

The Essenes were an extremely pious religious group that is associated with the community at Qumran where the Dead Sea Scrolls were found. These scrolls are evidence of the scholarly nature of this group, which maintained an extensive religious library, not just their own written works. This has led to the premature conclusion that certain Dead Sea scrolls define the group's practices or doctrines, but as research continues, what is evident is that they maintained an ancient library, or archive (Falk, p. 62) of variant viewpoints. A single scroll does not define the doctrine of the Essenes any more than a copy of a book on magic in a modern library defines the town as witches and warlocks.

This may account for the popular belief that the Essenes used a different calendar than their contemporaries. Falk (p. 69) writes that "the evidence involved is so contradictory and inconclusive that the issue does not lend itself to logical discussion."

What is known is that the Essenes, especially the Qumran group, withdrew from society in protest and had active conflict with the religious authorities. They withdrew into a purified community as revolutionists, awaiting divine intervention to destroy the evil social order.[33] The Essenes were obsessed with

33. Saldarini, 2001, p. 124

ritual purity even though they declined to attend Temple worship, objecting to the ruling Sadducean priesthood as imposters, a deviation from the Biblical requirements on lineage.

According to the historian Josephus, Essenes believed in the immortality of the soul that was merely chained to a body, but would be released incorporeal after death to attain higher existence-compare to Greek philosophy established by Plato. Other scholars discount Josephus' record:

> Josephus reported that the Essenes shared the belief in the immortality of the soul in the same way as the Greeks (War 2.154–155)...this is contrary to Hippolytus of Rome (about 170–236 CE) who reports that the Essenes acknowledge both that the flesh will rise again, and that it will be immortal (Refutation of All Heresies 9.27). (Bredin, 2003, p. 98)

Again, although some Essenes may have had the more "Greek" viewpoint, it did not characterize the entire sect.

Although the Pharisees are credited with the formation of a doctrine of Messiah, other sects such as the Essenes didn't derive such a clear-cut figure:

> No uniform Jewish expectation of a single eschatological figure existed in the 1st century. A majority expected the Messiah. But some pseudepigraphic books describe God's intervention without mentioning the anointed Davidic king; in parts of 1 Enoch, for example, the figure of the Son of Man, not the Messiah, embodies the expectations of the author. Essenes

at Qumran seem to have expected three figures: a prophet, a priestly messiah, and a royal messiah.[34]

Other myths about the Essenes have been debunked with progressing archaeological finds, including one that the communities had no women. What archaeology does prove beyond a shadow of a doubt is that Essenes were scrupulous in ritual purity, especially in water immersion.

## Scribes

Scribes, or *soferim*,[35] were not a sect of First Century Judaism, but more of an ancient religious profession. In an era of history where literacy was valuable, especially to Israelites who needed reliable copyists and interpreters of the Hebrew Scriptures, *soferim* provided those services. This profession was handed down through the generations, and Jewish surnames such as Sofer or Soper can indicate such an ancestor.

As the copyists of the Scriptures, scribes were "wise men," for they learned the Scriptures thoroughly in the process of transcribing perfect copies. If even a "jot or tittle" was miscopied or smudged, that leaf could not be stitched to the manuscript. A sofer had to be consulted if there was damage to a scroll, and only a sofer could repair scrolls. The soferim had a profession based on Biblical perfection in the transmission of the text and its language, Hebrew.

> ...the scribe as such is not of Pharisaic origin, that long before Pharisaism ever existed there were scribes both in the Jerusalem temple and also throughout the dispersion, and that the scribes gave a religious and philosophical aspect to Judaism... up to 70 A.D. there were always non-Pharisaic scribes who united the Law and wisdom...but as

34. Biblical Studies Press. (2006). The NET Bible First Edition Notes (Jn 1:19). Biblical Studies Press.

35. Sofer is singular for scribe; sefer means "book" in Hebrew. An easy way to remember the Hebrew title is to think of the scribes as human books.

wisdom provided fertile soil for the
development of sacral law on a
broader basis, so did Pharisaism
with its attempt to fulfil the Law
in everyday life...the scribe in his
capacity as a sofer, i.e., a guardian
and interpreter of the Torah, was
vitally necessary to the inner and
outer life of the perushim... (Kittel,
Bromiley & Friedrich, pp. 22–23)

Scribes were trusted and desired to validate any doctrines or teachings, for if the teaching deviated from the plain sense of the text, the scribes would not validate it.

## Jewish Literature and Teaching Tools

Another player in the gospels and letters of the New Testament is Jewish literature used as a teaching tool. Although not a sect or group, Jewish literature permeates the New Testament, often providing clarity to the listeners who shared a common literature. For instance, Jewish tradition handed down many details about Old Testament (TANAKH) characters. An example is the son of the Shunamite woman whom Elisha resurrected.[36] The resurrected son was believed to be the Prophet Jonah.

When Yeshua speaks of "the sign of Jonah," most Christians identify with three days and three nights in the belly of the fish. For a Jew, however, Jonah was known as one who was resurrected, which adds a layer of understanding. Yeshua was not only claiming he would be preserved alive for three days and three nights, but that he would literally be resurrected from the dead.

A sometimes-puzzling component handed down in the Jewish tradition is aggadah, which can be confusing to a non-Jew who is not sure how to categorize the aggadic stories of Judaism.

36. 2 Ki 4:35

Aggadah is an illustrative story that may use Biblical characters to teach a lesson, but the story is not found in Scripture. Parables such as Yeshua used are aggadah, helping the listener to form a concrete picture of a spiritual concept.

Here is the Jewish view of aggadah's role:

> As a rule, aggadah should not be taken literally; rather, it must be interpreted with the understanding that a higher truth is being alluded to—a truth that is beyond historical perspective, philological expression, or the dimensions of scientific observations. Agaddah speaks to that part of us that understands but cannot articulate what it understands. It allows us to go beyond the realms of the definable, perceivable, and demonstrable. In this sense, aggadah is a form of religious metaphor, a mirror that enables us to form mental images of the indescribable. (Ben Malka & Shahar, 2015, p. 11)

So whether Jonah was or was not the Shunamite's resurrected son, Yeshua appeals to the Jewish tradition. It adds to his message by associating his work with something already known.

The problem for the non-Jewish reader of the New Testament is the unfamiliarity with Jewish literature and aggadah. Sometimes the allusions are there, but since the reader does not know the story or tradition, it is not recognized for what it is. It would be hard to say, "Nice to see you again" if I'd never met you before. These ancient stories are not necessary to understanding the simple level of the text, but as in the case of the sign of Jonah, the depth and richness can be lost.

Sadly, Western-educated believers today do share a literature tradition that is sprinkled into the vocabulary. Most readers can define an Achilles' heel, narcissism, a Pandora's box, or even explain why a spacecraft would be named Apollo. Our shared literature comes from Greek mythology and the antics of their gods. The shared literature of the ancient Greek and Roman world does affect modern conversations, songs, literature, and symbols even today. For that reason, consider that the Jewish tradition, like a sect or group, may exert an influence into the New Testament Scriptures that is partially or completely lost on the non-Jewish reader.

# 5

## A TALE OF TWO HOUSES

The Pharisees were comprised of two schools, or "houses" of learning and practice. Understanding the wide differences between the Sadducees and Pharisees is only half of the key to understanding the gospel dialogues with Pharisees. The other half is understanding the sharp differences between the two schools of the Pharisees.

Each of the two houses of the Pharisees was founded by a scholar whose approach to the Scriptures and Oral Law defined his students. Both of these scholars were contemporaneous to one another, and roughly contemporaneous to Yeshua, slightly overlapping his generation. Hillel's religious leadership lasted from 30 BCE – 10 CE, his death occurring around 20 CE. Shammai was born around 50 BCE and died around 30 CE. Both leaders were prominent in the time of Yeshua's boyhood, and Shammai's leadership would have extended into Yeshua's adulthood. Shammai's school was pre-eminent until the destruction of the Temple in 70 CE.

## Shammai

Little is known about Shammai's personal life except that like Yeshua, he was a builder. He became the vice-president of the Great Sanhedrin during the time that Hillel was its president. During Yeshua's lifetime, Shammai's stricter legal rulings were more in favor, and his school held the greater influence over Hillel's until 70 CE.

Although in his religious views, Shammai was known to be strict, ironically, he is well known for his recommendation of having a friendly attitude toward all. His motto was "Make the study of the Torah your chief occupation; speak little, but accomplish much; and receive every man with a friendly countenance." (Pirkei Avot)

Shammai pushed away with his builder's "measuring rod" one of the Gentiles who asked to be converted to the faith of Abraham, for he scorned converts. Shammai accepted only wealthy, educated, and socially upward students. Most of his interpretations, applications, and rulings of Jewish law, except for marriage, were strict and literalist. Christians might say, "More *letter* than spirit," and Jews might say, "More *line* of the law."

Interestingly, Jewish sources predict that during the rule of Messiah, the stricter rulings of the House of Shammai will prevail once again. If this sounds outlandish to our grace-filled and highly-favored view of Messiah's reign, consider John's revelation of Messiah's rule:

> AND HE SHALL RULE THEM WITH A
> ROD OF IRON, AS THE VESSELS OF THE
> POTTER ARE BROKEN TO PIECES, as
> I also have received authority from
> My Father; TOOLS. (Re 2:27)

And she gave birth to a son, a male

child, who is to rule all the nations
with a rod of iron; and her child was
caught up to God and to His throne.
(Re 12:5)

From His mouth comes a sharp
sword, so that with it He may strike
down the nations, and He will rule
them with a rod of iron; and He
treads the wine press of the fierce
wrath of God, the Almighty. (Re
19:15)

Although Messiah has drawn down the Father's favor
on those who are His, it sounds as though Shammai's
wooden rod is rather puny compared to Messiah's
iron one!

### Hillel

The leader known as "Hillel the Elder" was known for
compassion, gentleness, patience, and his lenient
"spirit of the law" rulings. He also is known for the
"three converts," whom he accepted and taught.
Hillel received even the poorest students, for it is
believed that he was educated by two descendants
of converts. Hillel believed that salvation extended
even to the righteous Gentile.

Both Hillel and his disciples were humble enough
to study, and even incorporate, Shammai's better
rulings. Hillel may have been a woodcutter by
occupation, and he lived a simple life, teaching that
multiplied goods also multiplied trouble. Although
he was the great sage of his generation, sources
suggest that his wife did not appear to have even
kitchen help.

*Shammai, Hillel, and the Three Converts*

How the two scholars treated the "three converts" are the essence of the difference between Shammai and Hillel. According to the story, three Gentiles visited both Shammai and Hillel. Each non-Jew offers to convert and become Jewish under a specific condition:

Condition #1 Standing on One Foot – "Teach me the entire Torah while I'm standing on one foot."

Condition #2 Without the Oral Torah – "Convert me on the condition that you teach me only the Written Torah."

Condition #3 If I Can be the High Priest – "If you'll make me the High Priest, I'll convert."

Shammai and Hillel have different reactions to the three men. In summary, Shammai pushes away the Gentiles with his wooden measuring rod, and the rationale for his reactions are as follows:

**#1 Standing on One Foot** – No Easy, Greasy. There are no shortcuts to serving God. The unlimited knowledge of Torah and an omniscient God cannot be contained in a sentence or two. The Gentile does not "measure up" to Shammai's admission standards, and Shammai pushes him away with the rod.

**#2 Without the Oral Torah** – No Rugged Individualists. The convert cannot learn the doctrine of the resurrection with only the letter of the Torah. For instance, can you only accept the Constitution, but not the amendments and local laws of the United States, such as stop signs? (Shabbat 31a) The local stop sign doesn't "add" to the Constitution; instead, it "grows" a life-preserving application from the seed, the Constitution. Shammai merely pushes him away without the rod.

**#3 If I Can be the High Priest** – No Presumption. The Gentile had walked by a house of study and heard the Biblical passages describing the gold and jewels of the high priest's attire. Acceptance of the covenant is not based on elevating the individual over others or wearing external "play pretties." Again, Shammai pushes him away with the rod.

On the other hand, Hillel received each potential convert and put him to work learning the Scriptures. Hillel taught each convert by letting him discover the answers and his own presumption:

**#1 Standing on One Foot** – Hillel responds with the Golden Rule: "Whatever is hateful to you, don't do to your neighbor. The rest is commentary. Go and learn." Hillel's approach is to get to the essence and simplify...THEN study the details. He ignored the arrogance of the offer.

**#2 Without the Oral Torah** – Hillel teaches the potential convert the first four letters of the Hebrew alphabet so that he will be able to read the Hebrew text of the Torah: Alef, Beit, Gimel, Dalet. When the student returns the next day, Hillel teaches the letters in a different order, and the student protests. Hillel says, "If you rely on me to recognize the letters of the alefbet, then rely on me to explain how Torah is to be understood." An example is in the Torah itself (Dt 12:21), which reads: "...as I have instructed you." There are no written instructions, implying that Moses did receive some things orally to pass along. Private interpretation of Torah, which is prophecy, is dangerous and arrogant, and it separates the individual from the faith community. (1 Pe 1:20)

**#3 If I Can be the High Priest** – Hillel ignores the simple-minded request based on hearing teaching about beauty of the priestly garments. Hillel teaches "the ceremonies of royalty" until the Gentile discovers Numbers 3:10 & 18:7 in his studies, which define priests as physical descendants of Aaron. Hillel lets the individual discover his own romanticized presumption, not exactly true arrogance.

Hillel took the opportunity to take the Gentiles' interest, accept them, and teach them a few things, knowing that if they were serious about leaving polytheism, then they would grow past arrogance, presumption, or shallow motivations. He believed strongly in the many passages of the TANAKH that refer to righteous Gentiles, like Ruth and Rahab, who became converts to the faith of Abraham, Isaac, and Jacob.[37]

### Sometime Allies: Hillel and the Essenes

The Essenes (authors of the Dead Sea Scrolls) were closely allied with the House of Hillel. Some of Hillel's disciples left the school and joined the Essenes when the House of Shammai gained control of the Jewish community. Hagigah 2:2 of the Jerusalem Talmud "describes their exodus as a mission of conciliation to the Gentiles." (Falk, p. 140)

In the *Talmud*, the Essenes, Hillel, and Hillel's disciples were referred to as Hasidim; they were not called "Pharisees or scribes."[38] This may explain why the writers of the Gospels did not distinguish for the reader to which house of the Pharisees each particular speaker belonged. In the culture of the First Century Jews, the gospel reader may have assumed that a person identified as a "Pharisee" was likely a member of the House of Shammai. Although the students of the House of Hillel were Pharisees, the writers may have already begun distinguishing them from Shammai's House by de-emphasizing the title of Pharisee and emphasizing their *Hasidism*, a Hebrew word. Its verb form means:

> חסד: conduct oneself as *chasid* (loyal, faithful) 2 Sa 22:26/Ps 18:26.[39]

The noun form means:

> חסיד: one is chasid if he practices chesed: one who is faithful, devout:

37. Falk makes a reasonable case that the converts were discipled by Hillel in two different types of conversions: a *ger toshav* and *ger tzedek*. The one who merely wanted the simplicity of the commandments was converted to a "Noachide," or *ger tzedek*, responsible for the ethical, but not ritual, commandments of the Torah; the other two requested to be made a *ger toshav*, or full convert to the Jewish faith. This is based on Hillel's answer and Rashi's interpretation of "neighbor" as "God, one's fellow man, and the animal world." (p. 26-27)

38. Falk, pp. 114, 146

39. Holladay, 2000, p. 111.

1 Sa 2:9 & often of God Je 3:12.[40]

*Strong's Concordance* defines a Hasid as one who is kind and pious. In practice, the rulings of the House of Hillel were generally much more kind than the more literalist rulings of the House of Shammai. The lexicon cites 1 Samuel 2:9, which identifies a *hasid*:

> He will guard the feet of *his faithful ones*, but the wicked shall be cut off in darkness.[41]

A Hasid of the First Century is viewed as a charismatic individual, and according to famed Biblical critic Geza Vermes, the gospel accounts of Yeshua cast him as a Galilean Hasid:

> It is now, rightly, the case that we have been led to question the radical disjunction between Jesus and 1st century Judaism which used to be taken as a norm... Vermes investigates known categories, types of figures, manners of speech, messianic expectations and so on, from (circa) 1st century Judaism and compares their characteristics to gospel accounts of Jesus and His work. For Vermes, Jesus fits neatly into the analysis of a 'Galilean Hasid.'[42]

In the minds of New Testament scholars such as Vermes, Yeshua fit the mold of First Century Hasidim, the designation of the Hillelite Pharisees. Therefore, there is reason to read many, but *not all*, of the gospel references to Pharisees as members of the House of Shammai. Considering the time that lapsed between the events of the Gospels and their historical recording, blurring of the distinctions is to be expected. Writers often do not anticipate that their readers hundreds, and even thousands of years

40. ibid

41. 1 Sa 2:9

42. Torrance, 2006, p. 196.

after the events the writers record, will not have the firsthand knowledge of the political, economic, and religious realities of the generation.

## Sometime Allies: Shammai and the Zealots

Judas Iscariot (possibly from *sicarii*-assassins) is identified with the Zealots, a revolutionary sect that included a splinter group of assassins who carried hidden daggers to use against Romans and what they considered apostate Jews. Judas may not have been one of the sicarii, however, because one idea is that Iscariot refers to Kerioth, a region or town in Judea. Either explanation would identify him with the more ritually scrupulous and fervent Judeans.

If Judas was one of the Sicarii, a cadre of assassins among the nationalist Jewish Zealot rebels, his sect was sometimes allied with the House of Shammai. The Zealots' hatred of the Romans and Gentiles was an intersection with the House of Shammai. Josephus branded them "murderers" for their atrocities against fellow Jews who believed or practiced differently. Gamaliel the Elder, a grandson of Hillel, strongly denounced the founder of the Zealots, Judas the Galilean (not to be confused with Yeshua's disciple).

This strong denouncement of the Zealots by the House of Hillel partially stems from the "eighteen measures"[43] that Shammai introduced to create greater separation between Jew and Gentile. The Jerusalem Talmud records that the House of Hillel opposed these measures, for Hillel said,

> Be of the disciples of Aaron, one who loves peace, pursues peace, loves mankind, and brings them near to the Torah. (Pirkei Avot 1:12)

Shammai, however, was an isolationist, and during the debate over the eighteen measures, an unknown number of students from the House of Hillel were

43. Shabbat 13b

71

murdered. The evidence points to the Zealots, who were present at the time.[44] While the Shammaiites would not likely take up arms and murder their Hillelites opponents, the Zealots would.

It was likely the House of Shammai to whom Yeshua directed his accusations about even after traveling "over land and sea," only make a single proselyte, and then they "shut up the Kingdom of Heaven in men's faces." Yeshua points out that Shammai made it virtually impossible for "even the most sincere and virtuous Gentile to find his way to salvation."[45] The powerful move of the Holy Spirit among the proselytes in Acts Two validated Yeshua and Hillel's merciful acceptance of the sincere Gentiles. The House of Shammai would not have been happy with that event, nor would their sometimes-allies, the Zealots.

*House of Shammai and Seed of Satan*

The House of Shammai more frequently opposed Yeshua for his Hillel-like compassionate interpretations of the Torah. Luke 22:3 links Judas with Satan. The Talmud links the House of Shammai with Satan, or to use John's term, "synagogue of Satan." (Falk, p. 146) The differences between the two schools on prayer, feasts, and other practices, were sharp, so their synagogues were likely separate. Satan means "adversary."

Two passages in Revelation can be removed from First Century context to create stereotypes and reinforce ethnocentricity. Both passages mention the "synagogue of Satan," a First Century epithet describing those who distorted the Torah or Jewish law. Other similar expressions are "brood of vipers" or "serpents." John the Baptist called some of the Sadducees and Pharisees a brood of vipers when they came to him for immersion.[46]

The key is that John pointed out their lack of

44. Shabbat 1:4; Sukkah 28a; Bava Batra 134a

45. Falk, p. 123, Shabbat 31a

46. Mt 3:7-8

repentance, their departure from the written Torah. He mentions that they are fleeing the "wrath to come," which for the Sadducees, would have been only to flee the wrath of physical destruction by the Romans, for they did not believe in the resurrection of the soul to final judgment. The unrepentant among Pharisees were also true "serpents," denying the repentance required by their governing document, the TANAKH, or Old Testament Scriptures, just as the serpent first told Eve, "You shall not surely die" [if you sin].[47]

The Pharisees believed in a final judgment and wrath on the unrepentant, so not to live according to that Pharisaic vision was hypocritical. In that respect, any person who does not live according to the expectation of his or her faith can be called a serpent, or if that person associates with a like-minded, hypocritical group of people among his faith, then he is part of a brood, or nest, of vipers who preach one thing and practice another.

It is helpful to know that the Pharisees believed in and taught much about the "World to Come," or afterlife. [48] The righteous do not experience the torment of Sheol (hell). They are in "Abraham's bosom"[49] and "gathered to their people" in The Garden of Eden, and this is experienced immediately after death. This waiting period is distinguished from the rewards in the *Olam Haba*, or World to Come, after the resurrection and Messiah's Kingdom.

The wicked and intermediates descend to Sheol. According to Jewish tradition, the intermediates, or "lukewarm"[50] as Yeshua calls them, are purified and experience torment for up to twelve months, but repentance may shorten the term. They may then ascend to the Garden of Eden, but

> ...their subsequent afterlife experience is not in any way as supernal and blissful as that of

47. Ge 3:4

48. Some passages taken from *50,000 Degrees and Cloudy: A Better Resurrection* by the author to be released in 2019

49. This will be explained more completely in *50,000 Degrees and Cloudy: A Better Resurrection* and *The Cave of the Couples* in future BEKY Books.

50. Re 3:16

73

the righteous.  Such sinners, even
after they exit from Gehenna, are
granted post-mortem repose of a
lesser grade-that is, below that of the
righteous-hence the phrase '**at the
feet of the righteous.**' (Raphael, pp.
266-267)

This phrase "at the feet of the righteous" has a similar
phrase in the Book of Revelation:

He who is holy, who is true, who has
the key of David, who opens and
no one will shut, and who shuts and
no one opens, says this: 'I know your
**deeds.** Behold, **I have put before
you an open door which no one
can shut**, because you have a little
power, and **have kept My word**,
a nd have not denied My name.
Behold, I will cause those of the
**synagogue of Satan**, who say that
they are Jews and are not, but lie—**I
will make them come and bow
down at your feet, and make them
know that I have loved you.** (Re 3:7-
9)

It is very important for the reader to understand who
the "synagogue of Satan" was in the First Century.
Otherwise, the meaning of the passage will be
skewed and become anti-Semitic, which neither
the Father, Yeshua, nor John would tolerate.  The
synagogue of Satan message in Revelation is one of
*inclusion* of the righteous Gentiles, not damnation of
all Jews.

In a nutshell, the synagogue of Satan could refer
specifically to the First Century Pharisaical School of
Shammai, which rejected the inclusion of converts
from the nations.  It was called the seed of Satan
by the Pharisaical School of Hillel, of which Paul was

a member.  The Hillelite Pharisaic sect embraced the Gentile convert who wanted to be included in the nation of Israel, and they rejected the pride of the Shammaiites, or the "seed of Satan" that would damn Gentiles eternally to the prison of Sheol.  To Paul and the School of Hillel, excluding Gentile converts to the God of Abraham, Isaac, and Jacob was a very *un-Jewish* position.

John's Revelation is that the hypocrisy and selfishness of those who want to exclude righteous Gentiles will be exposed, and they will be surprised that their Garden experience is reduced in quality.  Instead of the high ("rich") position to which they believe they were entitled, the synagogue of Satan experiences a kind of poverty, or low position, at the feet of those who were only apparently impoverished before death.  John the Baptist points this out by reminding the hypocrites that being descended from Abraham[51] secures no one a death free of life's consequences.

In fact, calling them hypocrites implies that the authentic Pharisee is one walking in a desirable faith, for Strong's defines a hypocrite (G5273) as:

> *hypokrites*; from G5271; an actor
> under an assumed character (stage-
> player), i.e. (figuratively) a dissembler
> ("hypocrite")

A hypocrite is one only pretending to be a Pharisee, but he is an actor on a stage, lying about his true identity, for if he truly believed in judgment for one's sins and eternal reward or punishment, he would clean the inside of his heart as well as the "staged" behaviors to avoid Sheol.  He would be a Pharisee both inside and out.

In Revelation, the humble, but faithful, disciples find that once they enter the Garden, they are given the rich position to which the proud believed they would

51. Mt 3:9

be entitled.[52]   In fact, the righteous are given two crowns, one of which is mentioned in the other reference to the synagogue of Satan:

> The first and the last, **who was dead, and has come to life**, says this: '**I know your tribulation and your poverty (but you are rich)**, and the blasphemy by those who say they are Jews and are not, but are a **synagogue of Satan**. Do not fear what you are about to suffer. Behold, the devil is about to cast some of you into prison, so that you will be tested, and you will have tribulation for ten days. **Be faithful until death, and I will give you the crown of life**. He who has an ear, let him hear what the Spirit says to the churches. (Re 2:8-11)

52. The reader will recall Yeshua's warning not to pick the best place at a table lest the master of the banquet move him to a lower one. Instead, one should take a lower position and allow the master to move him higher. In Luke 11:43, Yeshua addresses the hypocrite mindset: "Woe to you Pharisees! For you love the best seat in the synagogues and greetings in the marketplaces." Yeshua reiterates the danger of coveting notice for one's piety and the higher position, which results in a lower position in the Kingdom. When one crowns himself on this earth, no crown remains for him in the Kingdom.

The crown of life is for authentic Jews as well as authentic Gentiles who have been grafted into Israel.  Sheol still has room for hypocrites who believe that by their political, religious, economic, social, or military positions they will inherit similarly high places in the Kingdom.  Yeshua teaches that faithfulness in spite of tribulation and poverty is true spiritual elevation and a crown in life after death.

The full context of turnabout in Revelation is from Isaiah, known among the Jewish sages as the Book of Consolation:

> The sons of those [Gentile nations] who afflicted you will come bowing to you,
>
> And all those who despised you will bow themselves at the soles of your feet... (Is 60:14).

76

This passage is in the "Consolations"[53] to Israel, assuring them that even after destruction and exile, they will be regathered and restored. The nations who tried to destroy Israel will instead bring their wealth and worship to the Holy City. To the extent that these hypocrites among the nations believed themselves to be agents of God in destroying and despising His people Israel, they will be lowered. In fact, the prophetic judgments on Israel will have a definite end-point. The hypocritical Gentile nations who justify persecution of Jews while they sin even more grievously will one day be stopped:

> Had I not feared the wrath of the enemy,
> lest their adversaries should misunderstand,
> Lest they should say, 'Our hand is high; and
> it is not the LORD who has done all this.' (Dt
> 32:27 NKJV)

These hypocrites will one day bow at the soles of Israel's feet. The good news is this: not every Gentile among the nations is a hypocrite any more than every Jew or Pharisee was a hypocrite! Within the Consolations to Israel is an assurance that the righteous Gentiles have a place of worship alongside Israel. The House of Shammai, whose students were called "seed of Satan," rejected the Gentile convert and his sacrifices on the altar. Isaiah predicted a House of Worship that welcomed all sincere believers.

> In Isaiah 40-66, then, monotheism is
> portrayed as a total and absolute
> phenomenon. But this does not lead
> to exclusiveness or intolerance. The
> foreigners are repeatedly promised
> access to the Temple and the divine
> service performed there–both as
> pilgrims and as practitioners (56:1-8;
> 66:18-21). The strident nature of these
> passages, with their bold assertion
> of priestly service by non-Israelites,
> strikes one as a polemical stance

53. The "Consolation" chapters are Isaiah 40-66. The annual mourning for the destructions of the two Temples that begins on the 17th of Tammuz comes to a halt on Tishah B'Av. The Shabbat immediately following is called *Shabbat Nachamu* (Shabbat of Comfort) because the Haftarah (reading from the Prophets) begins with the words "*Nachamu nachamu ami*" ("Comfort, comfort my people"). This begins a period of consolation and comfort leading up to Rosh Hashanah, the Jewish New Year.

in the postexilic community. 'As
for the foreigners ... who hold fast
to My covenant—I will bring them
to My sacred mount and let them
rejoice in My house of prayer. Their
burnt offerings and sacrifices shall
be welcome on My altar; for My
House shall be called a house of
prayer for all peoples" (56:6-7).
(Fishbane, quoting from *The JPS Bible
Commentary: Haftarot*)

Fishbane relates the ones who "despised you" to
Isaiah's earlier consolation prophecy of "a house of
prayer for all peoples" in Isaiah 56. So is the synagogue
of Satan the hypocritical, Shammai-leaning, Gentile-
excluding Jews, or is it the oppressive Gentile nations
who do not desire to worship the God of Israel in the
Holy City?  Yes.

### Moneychangers

Sacrificial gifts had to be designated when they
were brought to the Temple.  Many Gentiles did not
know to designate their sacrificial purchases from the
moneychangers.  This allowed the moneychangers
to mis-designate the money as "the Temple," or
"the Altar" for upkeep, and then the money was
not forwarded toward the sacrifice that the Gentile
had intended.   This practice was sanctioned
because Shammai's ruling allowed priests to refuse
them.  Instead, it could be pocketed and diverted,
sometimes to the Zealot priests, allies with the School
of Shammai.  The Talmud refers to these Zealots as
murderers and thieves, just as Yeshua called them a
"den of thieves"[54]:

And He began to teach and say to
them, 'Is not written, "'MY HOUSE
SHALL BE CALLED A HOUSE OF
PRAYER FOR ALL THE NATIONS'"?
But you have made it a ROBBERS'

54. Falk, p. 152-
153

DEN.' (Mk 11:17)

Shammai's doctrinal, and the Zealots' practical, reluctance to accept Gentile sacrifices (stopped completely by 66 AD) eventually led to the Temple's destruction when the Roman Emperor's sacrifice was declined.

# 6

## HOW BIBLICAL IS THE PHARISEES' ORAL LAW?

As a previous chapter pointed out, how do I say, "Nice to meet you" if I've never met you before? This is the challenge of non-Jews reading the New Testament. There is a wealth of Jewish custom and oral law within its pages, yet it is not recognized as such, for the average non-Jew is unfamiliar with those customs, traditions, and Jewish rabbinic applications of the written Torah. Ironically, this can lead readers of the gospels to conclude that First Century Jews were just plain mean when Yeshua is actually pointing out that a Pharisaic interpretation is correct.

The parable of the man on the road to Jericho alludes to a rabbinic law. It is the obligation of the priests, according to Jewish Oral Law, to attend to the wounded or dead who have no one else to care for them.[55] Although exempted from caring for the dead of immediate family, if there is no one else to

55. Munk, 1992, p. 256

honor the dead, then a Levite, a Kohen (priest), or even the Kohen HaGadol (High Priest) must do so.

The written Torah prohibits a priest from making himself unclean to tend to the dead of his own family. It is very specific, and it assumes that other family members can carry out the duties, but the "Pharisaic" oral law recognizes the spirit of the Torah is kindness. It answers the unwritten question, "What if no one else is there to help?" The Pharisaic answer is that even the High Priest is obligated to bury a corpse or tend to the wounded if no one else can, i.e., exactly the situation Yeshua presents in the parable.

Most of the priests in Yeshua's day were Sadducees who did not follow the Oral Law. A priest had to come from a certain Levitical clan. "Scholars were Pharisees, whereas among the chief priests and elders many were Sadducees."[56] This would be why the priest passed by a wounded and dying man. The Samaritans also followed the letter of the Torah, not the Oral Law. The Pharisees, however, followed Oral Law and ruled that a priest and Levite must sometimes make himself unclean in order to restore purity to the common Israelite. Their rationale is that this is typified by the sacrifice of the red heifer.

The one man who burned the red heifer made himself unclean, yet the ashes became ashes of purification available to the whole community. This is a picture of Messiah Yeshua. Because he voluntarily walked into the realm of uncleanness for the benefit of all Israel, the fiery Torah that was within Yeshua purified the flesh. It is available to make the whole community clean.

The Jericho road where the parable's robbery and beating took place has a Biblical history. Jerichoites assisted in repairing the walls of Jerusalem in Nehemiah 3:1-2:

56. Cohn, 1977, p. 26

> Then Eliashib the high priest rose up
> with his brethren the priests, and
> they built the sheep gate; they
> sanctified it, and set up the doors
> of it; even unto the tower of Meah
> they sanctified it, unto the tower of
> Hananeel. And next unto him built
> the men of Jericho. It was the high
> priests, the Levites, **and the people
> of Jericho** who repaired the door for
> the sheep into Jerusalem.

Jericho-dwellers played a part in repairing the breaches in the walls and gates of Jerusalem, the city of the Biblical feasts and holy things. As there were two blind men healed in Jericho,[57] there were two coins given to the innkeeper by the Good Samaritan in Yeshua's example of a good neighbor on the road to Jericho. Rahab was the harlot who received and joined herself to Israel in Jericho, and she was also an innkeeper; she harbored two spies who brought redemption to her house in the wall of the city.

In these examples, there are those who honor the Father and Israel with healing and repair, and there are those who rob the honor due the Father and Israel. The Levite and priest dishonored a dying man when the very essence of their positions in Israel was to teach life and soul repair. The Good Samaritan, even though an Israelite of mixed ancestry and defective in his belief and observance, was obedient to the Torah of kindness, going beyond the letter of the Torah as the Oral Law required.

The Samaritan bound up the wounds of the one who was left half-dead. According to the Oral Law of the Pharisees, one who is in the process of dying is still treated as though he will live. The Samaritan is acting out of character with his religion's dogma when he shows mercy and reveals himself to be the "neighbor,"[58] the one honoring a dying man with

57. Mt 20:29-30

58. According to Rashi's commentary to Genesis, portion *Vayeitze*, "neighbor" includes God, people, and animals.

the expectation of life. Because the priest and Levite expected the man to die, they dishonored his life in order to remain ritually clean for service. Although there were many other priests and Levites who could have carried on with the ritual duties in the Temple, the dying man needed immediate attention.

Since many of the priests and Levites were Sadducees, however, they did not accept the Oral Law of the Pharisees that recognized saving a life had precedence over ritual purity.

## The Rabbinic Fence

Among the Pharisaic rabbis, "building fences around the Torah" was the practice of teaching an "Oral Torah," to protect the individual from breaking the written Torah. The "fences" were additional observations and practices as safeguards, or Oral Law. The reasoning was that the extra fence would slow down or stop disobedience before it hit the real fence, the written Word.

Dr. Kathleen Troost-Kramer (2016) suggests:

> One of the most famous, and misunderstood, 'fences' that Jesus constructed around the Torah is his teaching on anger and murder, found in the Sermon on the Mount in Matt. 5:21-22: 'You have heard that the ancients were told, "'You shall not commit murder'" and "'Whoever commits murder shall be liable to the court.'" But I say to you that everyone who is angry with his brother shall be guilty before the court; and whoever says to his brother, "'You good-for-nothing,'" shall be guilty before the supreme court; and whoever says, "'You fool,'" shall be guilty enough to go

into the fiery hell.

If a person does not put a fence around her strong emotions, then the anger, resentment, and bitterness can grow to the point that actual murder is contemplated and accomplished. Because Bible readers are conditioned to accept that angry emotions need to be curbed, it is easy to accept Yeshua's fence. Bible students are less conditioned to accept a Pharisaical fence.

Dr. Troost-Kramer defines other "fences around the Torah in Jesus' Sermon on the Mount:

> Vows: Mt 5:33-37
>
> Justice: Mt 5:38-42, 38-42
>
> Sexual Morality: Mt 5:27-30
>
> Mercy: Mt 5:43-48

> All of these passages begin with the words 'You have heard it said...' followed by a commandment, then 'But I say to you...' and Jesus' 'fence.' This construction does not indicate that Jesus is changing the commandment, but that he is reinforcing it by providing a 'fence.' He is giving his disciples practical advice for their behavior that will help them to keep the commandment, not replace it with something else or something new. (ibid)

Yeshua taught his students "Oral Law" similar to the other Pharisaic proto-rabbis of his day. It would be interesting to hear a conversation between Yeshua and the potential Gentile convert #2, the one who wanted to be taught only the written Torah without the Oral Law. Would that Gentile jump up offended and stalk away from the Sermon on the Mount? If we thought that Yeshua's fences were "rabbinic" or "Pharisaic," would we?

It is important not to place horns on the heads of Pharisees when we place a halo on Yeshua for identical, or nearly-identical statements. In *Truth, Tradition, or Tare: Growing in the Word,* the author presents an easy framework for decoding which "fences" Yeshua condemned and why. Sometimes fences make good neighbors.

# 7

## ESCHATOLOGY

What differentiates Pharisee from Essene and Sadducee, and Pharisee from Pharisee is *eschatology*.

---

*Eschatos* = Greek word meaning "end, final, or last,"

joined with ▼

*Logos* = reasoning about, discussion of

---

"Eschatology is a branch of theology that discusses the events that lie at the very end of history and of time as we know and experience it."[59] The particular concern of eschatology that distinguished the Pharisees from other First Century Judaisms was the resurrection of the dead. Rabbi Nathan Cardozo cites key passages from the Prophets that establish the doctrine of resurrection:

59. Gillman, 2015, p. 21

The revival of the dead, for Jews,
is more than a metaphor; it has
taken on substance and form in our
tradition. Isaiah prophesied:

'Your dead will live; their corpses will
rise. You who lie in the dust, awake
and shout for joy, for your dew is
as the dew of the dawn, and the
earth will give birth to the departed
spirits. Come, my people, enter into
your rooms and close your doors
behind you; hide for a little while
until indignation runs its course. For
behold, the Lord is about to come
out from His place to punish the
inhabitants of the earth for their
iniquity; and the earth will reveal her
bloodshed and will no longer cover
her slain.'

This took on more concrete imagery
in Ezekiel:

'Behold, I will cause breath to enter
you that you may come to life. I will
put sinews on you, make flesh grow
back on you, cover you with skin
and put breath in you that you may
come alive; and you will know that I
am The Lord.'

From a few lines of lyrical and
allusive prophecy, whole worlds
have taken shape. We have formed
a picture of what the Revival of the
Dead will entail. This picture is based
largely on the speculations of our
sages during the time of the Second
Temple and—even more—after the
destruction of Jerusalem and the
beginnings of a long exile. (quoted in

Ben Malka and Shahar, 2015, p. 10)

The problem with the other major sect, Sadducees, is that they accepted only the first five books of the Bible as authoritative. The resurrection of the dead is one of those doctrines that would be difficult to derive only from those books, especially in foresight, not the hindsight that Christians have today.

The proto-rabbinic Pharisees and later rabbis found resurrection proof texts for their belief in the resurrection.

> R. Meir said, 'Whence do we know resurrection from the Torah? From the verse, "'Then shall Moses and the children of Israel sing this song unto the Lord'" (Ex 15:1). Not *sang* but *shall sing* is written: thus, resurrection is taught in the Torah.' (Babylonian Talmud, Sandhedrin 91b)

The "rabbinic" or "Mishnaic" period of Jewish history followed the destruction of the Second Temple. According to tradition, at that time a *bat kol*, or heavenly voice, spoke that the decisions of the House of Hillel would prevail. Mercy, not strict judgment. These successors of the Pharisees designated themselves rabbis, not Pharisees. In the rabbinic era following the destruction of the Second Temple, interpretations of Scripture naturally allude to pre-destruction ones. Yeshua made this statement referring to Hosea 6:6:

> But go and learn what this means: 'I DESIRE COMPASSION, AND NOT SACRIFICE,' for I did not come to call the righteous, but sinners.' (Mt 9:13)

In context, Yeshua was challenged by a group of Pharisees (most likely Shammaiites) for eating with tax collectors and sinners. With only half the story, this is a valid challenge, for one is to avoid the very appearance of evil, a "fence" upheld by Paul. [60] Prior to the meal, however, Yeshua called to Matthew to come, "*Follow* me." Leave your present station and attach yourself to a new life. Repent. If one has no contact with sinners, then how can they be instructed in the steps of repentance?

In Shammai's world, the Jewish sinner, like the Gentile, is avoided completely. The sinner is sacrificed for the messenger's purity and spotless reputation. The compassionate messenger, however, perceives in the sinner or in the tax collector who takes advantage of the poor a willingness to change, to follow a new path. The compassionate messenger turns aside to instruct the sinner in repentance. The more sinners who repent, the fewer sin sacrifices necessary. The more repentant, the more compassion that *baal teshuvah*[61] will show to others in his work, family, and other spheres of influence. Ben-Malka illustrates the essence of repentance:

> Atonement. *Kapparah*. But what is kapparah?
>
> 'What does the word sound like?' asked Rav Ish-Shalom.
>
> I was unsure what he was after.
>
> 'Cover,' he said. 'It sounds like the word *cover*. So think of it as *covering over* the harmful effects of a wrong act. The act is still part of the fabric of the universe, but the outgoing ripples that carry the ill effects are damped down.' (Ben Malka, p. 33)

Sin does have consequences that ripple out even to successive generations. By repenting, Yeshua taught, atonement is made, and the consequences of a sinful life are contained. God's forgiveness

60. 1 Th 5:22

61. Master of Return/ Repentance, a person who returns to God from a life of transgression. "Teshuvah"... can mean many things—return to purity, healing, rebuilding a sense of worth— all of which are inner processes, things felt and experienced...In Teshuvah, we... acknowledge our mistakes; we experience regret, understanding the full import of what we have done and mourning the consequences. We become someone else, someone who even if brought to exactly the same circumstances, would not make the same mistake again." (Ben Malka & Shahar, p. 39)

helps more than the sinner, it helps those who suffer or would suffer from the sinner's transgressions, both past and potential.

> Once Rabban Yohanan Ben Zakkai and Rabbi Joshua were walking by the ruins of the Temple. Rabbi Joshua said, 'Woe to us that the place where atonement for the sins of Israel was made has been destroyed!'

> But Rabban Yohanan Ben Zakkai replied, 'Do not be grieved, my son. We have a means of atonement that is just as effective. And what is it? *Gemilut hassadim*—acts of loving-kindness, as it is said, "'For I desire *chesed*—loving-kindness—and not sacrifice!'" (Hosea 6:6). (Avot d'Rabbi Natan 4:21)

In the preceding examples, later rabbis acknowledge what Yeshua quoted from Hosea a generation earlier, that all sin and need atonement. How can one demonstrate a change of heart? Acts of compassion. How did Yeshua say to change hearts? Acts of compassion. Those acts of compassion create ripple effects that in turn reduce sin in the world, covering a multitude of potential sins. "Every action in this world, every word, every thought, has an effect. But the actor is also acted upon by his action. The condition on which you are allowed to make a change in the world is that the world changes you as well."[62]

These later rabbis demonstrate the more compassionate worldview of the House of Hillel, not the exclusivity and self-isolation of the House of Shammai. The compassion exerted today can affect the quality of post-mortem life in the resurrection for many, even the nations:

62. Ben Malka, p. 34

91

And **they sang the song of Moses**,
the bond-servant of God, and the
song of the Lamb, saying, 'Great
and marvelous are Your works, O
Lord God, the Almighty. Righteous
and true are Your ways, King of the
nations!' (Re 15:3)

The message is transmitted to John in the context of
rabbinic expectation concerning the resurrection
of the dead in the Song of Moses: "Not *sang* but
*shall sing* is written: thus, resurrection is taught in the
Torah." A case may be made for the entire Book of
Revelation as a merging of the Torah and rabbinic
expectation, then building upon hints and the more
explicit words of the Prophets and Writings.

Raba said, 'Whence is resurrection
derived from the Torah? From
the verse, "'May Reuben live and
not die'" (Dt 33:6) meaning, *may
Reuben live*, in this world, *and not
die*, in the next.' (Sanhedrin 92a)

These texts were disputed by Sadducees because
they did not think the text supported the resurrection.
Since Sadducees disregarded the authority of the
Prophets and Writings along with the Oral Torah,
then they could discard Daniel, Job, and Isaiah's
resurrection passages.

The Pharisaic rabbis, however, offered these three
references to resurrection from the TANAKH as
summary arguments for their eschatology:

| Torah | Prophets and Writings |
|---|---|
| See now that I, I am He, and there is no god besides Me; It is **I who put to death and give life.** I have wounded and it is I who heal. And there is no one who can deliver from My hand. Dt 32:39 | Your dead will live; their corpses will **rise**. You who lie in the dust, **awake** and **shout** for joy, for your **dew** is as the dew of the dawn. And the earth will give birth to the departed spirits. Is 26:19<br><br>Many of those who **sleep** in the dust of the ground **will awake**, these to everlasting life, but the others to disgrace and everlasting contempt. Da 12:2 |

The more extensive list of texts includes extra-Biblical literature as well:

| TANAKH | PSEUDEPIGRAPHAL WORKS |
|---|---|
| Isaiah 25-26<br>Job 19:26<br>1 Samuel 25:29<br>Ezekiel 37<br>Daniel 10-12<br>*2 Maccabees 7<br><br>*Catholic Bibles | Enoch 91-92<br>Fourth Ezra 7:32<br>Sibyline Oracles IV:180<br>Testament of Benjamin 10:6-8 |

**What About Judgment?**

Pharisees believed that judgment accompanied the resurrection of the dead, some to eternal reward, and some to punishment. Their proof text is:

...the life [soul, *nefesh*] of my lord will

be bound up in the bundle of life [*ha-chaim*] in the care of the Lord; but He will fling away the life [soul, *nefesh*] of your enemies as from the hollow of a sling. (1 Sa 25:29)

The wicked souls are slung away from those first separated and then bundled together to life. Yeshua mentions such a process in the gospels:

'Strive to enter through the narrow door; for many, I tell you, will seek to enter and will not be able. Once the head of the house gets up and shuts the door, and you begin to stand outside and knock on the door, saying, "'Lord, open up to us!'" then He will answer and say to you, "'I do not know where you are from.'" Then you will begin to say, "'We ate and drank in Your presence, and You taught in our streets'"; and He will say, "'I tell you, I do not know where you are from; **DEPART FROM ME**, ALL YOU EVILDOERS.'"

In that place, there will be weeping and gnashing of teeth when you see Abraham and Isaac and Jacob and all the prophets in the kingdom of God, but yourselves being **thrown out**. And they will come from east and west and from north and south, and will recline at the table in the kingdom of God. And behold, some are last who will be first and some are first who will be last.' **Just at that time some Pharisees approached, saying to Him, "'Go away, leave here, for Herod wants to kill You.'"** (Lk 13:24-31)

94

This Pharisaic interaction with Yeshua can be explained in two contexts, the resurrection of the dead, and the Pharisees' desire to protect a like-minded preacher from Herod's soldiers. First, Yeshua teaches death and resurrection to the Garden, a Pharisaic, Bible-based doctrine:

> 1. "...there will be weeping and gnashing of teeth **when you see Abraham** and Isaac and Jacob and all the prophets in the kingdom of God, but yourselves being thrown out."

Yeshua preaches that regret occurs when the dead see the **living** patriarchs and prophets, whom the Sadducees believed were eternally dead. Along with realization that human souls are immortal comes the realization that they are being flung exactly where they expected to go, away from eternal "life." Even those from the nations who looked for resurrection are judged, rewarded, and included in the living "bundle." Hillelites would have prepared the audience with this doctrine, for they welcomed converts from the nations.

> 2. "Just at that time," "The Pharisees" warned Yeshua that Herod's soldiers were looking for Yeshua to put him to death.
>
> a. If "the Pharisees" truly sought to take Yeshua's life, then they would not have taken steps to preserve it. They would have let Judean civil government take the credit/blame for killing Yeshua.
>
> b. Which Pharisees wanted to protect him? Most likely those from the School of Hillel. Yeshua upheld their practical rulings most

of the time, i.e., walled-city *eruv.* In Matthew 9:6, Yeshua permits the lame man to pick up his bed and walk. Per Hillel, such an action is not a Sabbath-breaking sin. The wall of the city makes an *eruv*, a Sabbath boundary around Jerusalem. Within that boundary, one may carry certain non-commercial burdens on the Sabbath, especially if the person carried the item and placed it without intent to break the Sabbath. The paralytic would have had no expectation of healing until it occurred; therefore, he was "legal" on two counts with Hillelite Pharisees.

Yeshua affirms the Pharisaic doctrine of eternal reward and punishment:

Let the one who does wrong, still do wrong; and the one who is filthy, still be filthy; and let the one who is righteous, still practice righteousness; and the one who is holy, still keep himself holy. Behold, I am coming quickly, and **My reward is with Me, to render to every man according to what he has done**. I am the Alpha and the Omega, the first and the last, the beginning and the end. Blessed are those who wash their robes, so that they may have the right to the **tree of life**, and may enter by the gates into the city. **Outside** are the dogs and the sorcerers and the immoral persons and the murderers and the idolaters, and everyone who loves and practices lying. (Re 22:10-15)

There are other examples of Yeshua's and Paul's

identification with Pharisaic interpretation:

> Mark 12:18-27 & Matthew 22:23-
> 33. Sadducees challenge Yeshua
> on resurrection, the essence of his
> mission. Yeshua cites Exodus 3:6
> and says, "He is God, not of the
> dead, but of the living; you are
> quite wrong." To Yeshua, the Torah
> taught resurrection, a doctrine of the
> Pharisees.

> In Acts 23:6-7, the Apostle Paul
> declares: "I am a Pharisee, a son of
> Pharisees; I am on trial concerning
> the hope of the resurrection of the
> dead."

Yeshua's central message of forgiveness of sin and resurrection of the dead was not unusual or objectionable to the Pharisees or their adherents. "A central belief in their [the Pharisees'] reading of Judaism is a composite doctrine of the afterlife which includes both bodily resurrection and spiritual immortality."[63] This doctrine was in dispute among First Century Jews. It was rejected by Sadducees who controlled the Temple, and therefore they greatly controlled Jewish tax money. Disbelief in resurrection had economic tentacles attached to Rome. Other sects rejected a bodily resurrection, opting for a disembodied spiritual existence.

Yeshua clears up the question in his post-resurrection appearance to the disciples:

> But they were startled and
> frightened and thought that they
> were seeing a spirit. And He said to
> them, 'Why are you troubled, and
> why do doubts arise in your hearts?
> See My hands and My feet, that it
> is I Myself; touch Me and see, **for a**

63. Gillman, p. 121

> **spirit does not have flesh and bones
> as you see that I have**.' And when
> He had said this, He showed them
> His hands and His feet. While they
> still could not believe it because of
> their joy and amazement, He said
> to them, 'Have you anything here
> to eat?' They gave Him a piece of a
> broiled fish; and He took it and ate it
> before them. (Lk 24:37-43)

Yeshua overturns the eschatological doctrines of the Essenes and Sadducees. He affirms the faith of the Pharisees.

Q: So why did Yeshua have so many conflicts with the Pharisees?

A: Sometimes, confusing dialogue exchanges. It's not Pharisees.

> So Jesus was saying to **those Jews
> who had believed Him**, 'If you
> continue in My word, then **you are
> truly disciples of Mine**; and you will
> know the truth, and the truth will
> make you free.' (Jn 8:31-32)

Keep reading, however, and it sounds as though they DIDN'T believe him.

> **They** answered and said to Him,
> 'Abraham is our father.' Jesus said
> to them, 'If you are Abraham's
> children, do the deeds of Abraham.
> But as it is, **you are seeking to kill
> Me**, a man who has told you the
> truth, which I heard from God; this
> Abraham did not do. You are doing
> the deeds of your father.' (Jn 8:39-
> 40)

So did the Jews who believed Yeshua suddenly want to kill him? Or was he speaking to believers, as the context indicates, when he is interrupted by nonbelievers? The reader has to identify who "they" are, unbelievers.

> Why do **you** not understand what I am saying? It is because **you** cannot hear My word. **You** are of your father the devil, and **you** want to do the desires of your father. (Jn 8:43-44)

> 'If I speak truth, why do **you not believe** Me? He who is of God hears the words of God; for this reason **you** do not hear them, because **you** are not of God.' **The Jews answered** and said to Him, "'Do **we** not say rightly that You are a Samaritan and have a demon?'" (Jn 8:46-48)

There were two distinct groups of Jews: Jews who believed him, and Jews who didn't. Yeshua defends the Jews who believed. But who are the "you" Jews who didn't believe him and wanted to kill him?

> **The Jews** said to Him, 'Now we know that You have a demon. **Abraham died**, and **the prophets also**; and **You say**, "'If anyone keeps My word, **he will never taste of death**.'" Surely You are not greater than our father **Abraham, who died**? **The prophets died too**; whom do You make Yourself out to be?' (Jn 8:52-53)

Which group of Jews rejected life after death and believed only God was immortal? Sadducees.

> 'Your father Abraham rejoiced to see My day, and he saw it and was glad.' So **the Jews** said to Him, 'You

are not yet fifty years old, and have You seen Abraham?' Jesus said to them, 'Truly, truly, I say to you, **before Abraham was born, I am.' Therefore they picked up stones to throw at Him**, but Jesus hid Himself and went out of the temple. (Jn 8:56-59)

The Jews who believe Yeshua fade from the dialogue early. The conversation with *unbelievers* continues, Yeshua defending the "true disciples'" and believers' faith in resurrection. They continue in the Word he speaks because they believe in resurrection to judgment and eternal reward. Knowing who "the Jews," "you," and "they" are is found in the context and knowing the eschatological beliefs of First Century Sadducees and Pharisees.

Q: So why did Yeshua have so many conflicts with the Pharisees?

A: Sometimes the "house" of the Pharisee isn't supplied. You are expected to know by the Pharisee's questions and answers.

### Example

Fill in the denomination:

"Do you believe 'once saved, always saved'?

"Do you believe if you're not baptized, you're not saved?"

"Do you believe in purgatory?"

"Do you believe you must speak in tongues if you're saved?"

"Do you believe in predestination?"

The reader can probably fill in one or more Christian denominations as most likely to generate each of the preceding questions. The question reflects doctrine and eschatological beliefs. Historically, the differences in beliefs have caused Christians to brand one another "heretics." If we were to read sample dialogues among those groups, it would be fairly easy to guess the denominational influence of the speakers. Likewise, First Century readers would read into Yeshua's dialogues with his audiences and challengers the particular eschatological beliefs of those involved.

# 8

## JUDEA AND THE JEWS

In the four gospels, "The Jews" figure prominently, and usually negatively, in the narratives. In this case, it is good to notice that the references are negative, for they draw attention to the perplexing boundaries, overlaps, and intersections of First Century "Judaisms" as well as economic, political, geographic, and religious divides among Jews.

The chart below is a hyper-simplistic portrayal of different groups that have similar, overlapping, or dissimilar religious, economic, political, and militaristic beliefs and goals in the First Century. In fact, it would be quite a mess to show how each of the sub-groups overlap! Each produced its own literature, political methods of coping with Greece and Roman domination, and attitudes toward one another.

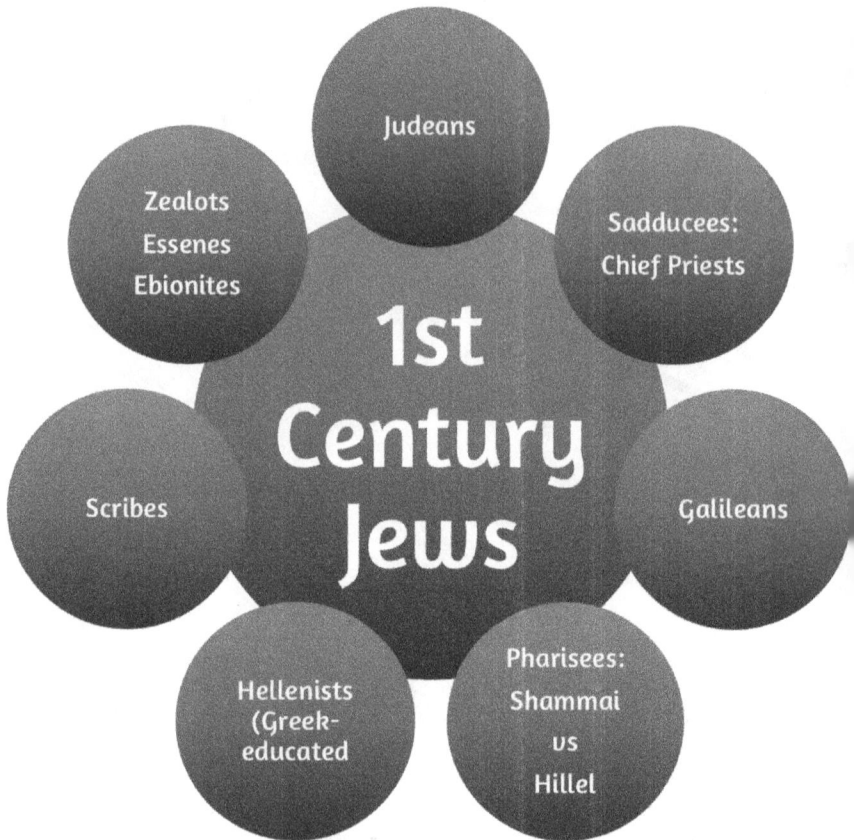

Figure 5

Those attitudes ranged from tolerance and collaboration to intense suspicion or hatred... and these are just the Jewish identities. It doesn't include such groups as the Romans, Idumeans, or Samaritans, who also figure prominently in the Gospels. No wonder so many Bible students throw up their hands and say, "Pharisees are hypocrites and Jews are mean!" Children typically learn more about American history than Biblical history, and it's up to the student to acquire that background knowledge.

Over-simplifications are not helpful, nor are they

truthful. For instance, because everyone knows from Yeshua's parable that a certain Samaritan was good, *all* Samaritans must have been good! After all, out of ten lepers, the only one who thanked Yeshua for his teaching was a Samaritan.[64]

## Just How Good Were the Samaritans?

There was a very good reason why the Jews were suspicious and avoided Samaritans. Their past history included an attempt to have Alexander the Great destroy Jerusalem,[65] and it was only through a great miracle that the evil plan was overturned. Other contexts tell the reader that Samaria had problems with sorcery and demonic possession (Acts 8), which might be why "The Jews" who were upset with Yeshua's teaching accused him of being a Samaritan and having a demon.[66]

Yeshua warned his disciples not to teach in Samaritan cities or the cities of the Gentiles (Mt 10:5). The Samaritans despised Jews because they worshiped in Jerusalem instead of a mountain in Samaria, Gerizim:

> He sent messengers on ahead of Him, and they went and entered a village of the Samaritans to make arrangements for Him. **But they did not receive Him, because He was traveling toward Jerusalem.** When His disciples James and John saw this, they said, 'Lord, do You want us to command fire to come down from heaven and consume them?' (Lk 9:52-54)

It was only after his resurrection, which was preached to the "Jew first," that the apostles began to go into all the earth, including Samaria. Samaria was neither full of Good Samaritans, nor was it inhabited only by sorcerers, demons, and adulteresses. Like all other

64. Lk 17:16

65. See Maccabees 1 & 2, where Samaritans are called "Cuthean."

66. Jn 8:48

105

people and religious groups, there was a mixture.

Galilee in the north of the Holy Land was a very distinct location from Judea, where the holy city Jerusalem was located. In its history, political status, culture, and even economics,[67] it was as different from the southern province of Judea as rural Alabama is from New York City. Galileans were known for their independence, and their religious practices were not always in unity with the Judeans', nor were their social and legal customs. Generally, they were lax in orthodoxy, but full of fire for their causes.

R. T. France, in his commentary on *The Gospel of Matthew*,[68] writes that modern readers of the New Testament often know little about the geopolitical world of First Century Palestine. It is commonly assumed that "the Jews" were one community living in the Holy Land. But, he says, "this is a gross distortion of the historical and cultural reality."

France summarizes seven differences:

- Racially, the area of the former Northern Kingdom of Israel had had, ever since the Assyrian conquest in the eighth century B.C., a more mixed population, within which more conservative Jewish areas (like Nazareth and Capernaum) stood in close proximity to largely pagan cities, of which in the first century the new Hellenistic centers of Tiberias and Sepphoris were the chief examples.
- Geographically, Galilee was separated from Judea by the non-Jewish territory of Samaria, and from Perea in the southeast by the Hellenistic settlements of Decapolis.
- Politically, Galilee had been under separate administration from Judea during almost all its history since the tenth century B.C. (apart from a period of "reunification" under the Maccabees), and in the time

67. Elliott-Binns, p. 25

68. NICNT, 2007

of Jesus it was under a (supposedly) native Herodian prince, while Judea and Samaria had, since A.D. 6, been under the direct rule of a Roman prefect.

- Economically, Galilee offered better agricultural and fishing resources than the more mountainous territory of Judea, making the wealth of some Galileans the envy of their southern neighbors.
- Culturally, Judeans despised their northern neighbors as country cousins, their lack of Jewish sophistication being compounded by their greater openness to Hellenistic influence.
- Linguistically, Galileans spoke a distinctive form of Aramaic whose slovenly consonants (they dropped their aitches!) were the butt of Judean humor.
- Religiously, the Judean opinion was that Galileans were lax in their observance of proper ritual, and the problem was exacerbated by the distance of Galilee from the temple and the theological leadership, which was focused in Jerusalem.

The result, France says, is that

> ...even an impeccably Jewish Galilean in first-century Jerusalem was not among his own people; he was as much a foreigner as an Irishman in London or a Texan in New York. His accent would immediately mark him out as 'not one of us,' and all the communal prejudice of the supposedly superior culture of the capital city would stand against his claim to be heard even as a prophet, let alone as the 'Messiah,' a title which, as everyone knew, belonged to Judea (cf. John 7:40-42).

Judeans considered themselves the "Hebrews of Hebrews."[69] It was only in Judea that rabbis could be ordained or the Sanhedrin could convene, and there were more schools of religious learning in Judea than in Galilee. In Judea, the great scholars were the Pharisees, yet the chief priests and elders were Sadducees and dominated the numbers of the Sanhedrin.[70] A Biblical example is in Matthew 21:23:

> When He entered the temple,
> the chief priests and the elders of
> the people came to Him while He
> was teaching, and said, 'By what
> authority are You doing these things,
> and who gave You this authority?'

Because rabbinic ordination was performed only in Judea, the "chief priests and elders," denoting the Sadducees, demanded the Galilean rabbi's ordaining authority.

Generally, the Judeans spoke of their favored position in the formerly Greek, and then Roman Empire relative to Syria (Damascus), "beyond Jordan," Galilee, and then Judea/Jerusalem. The Gospels reflect this awareness:

> The news about Him spread
> throughout all **Syria**; and they
> brought to Him all who were ill,
> those suffering with various diseases
> and pains, demoniacs, epileptics,
> paralytics; and He healed them.
> Large crowds followed Him from
> **Galilee** and the Decapolis and
> **Jerusalem and Judea** and from
> **beyond the Jordan**. (Mt 4:24–25)

69. Edersheim, p. 68

70. Cohn, pp. 26, 30

71. Edersheim, p. 68

The Judeans condescendingly referred to "Judeans as the grain, the Galileans as straw, and those beyond Jordan as chaff."[71] Lest we create an

108

artificial divide, the English translation of "the Jews" can also mean Galileans. Jews are still Jews as Hakola quotes from Reed:

> The term Jewish is thoroughly
> appropriate for the inhabitants
> of Galilee in the first century....
> Galilean Jews had a different social,
> economic, and political matrix
> than Jews living in Judaea or the
> Diaspora...but they were what we
> should call Jewish. (Hakola, 2005, p.
> 11)

The Jews of the Holy Land were all Jews, including Galileans, but the term could also specifically refer to religious Jews living in Judea, the seat of Jewish culture and learning. Again, this does not mean that the Galilean Jews had no culture or learning, but it was a matter of degree.

The friendlier climate, soil, and other natural resources of the Galilee, such as fish, afforded the Galileans greater economic opportunities to derive an income from the land, whereas Judean farming and commerce was more challenged, so the Temple in Jerusalem was a great "religious tourist" attraction then just as it is today. Converts and Jewish pilgrims from other countries visited Jerusalem for the three annual feasts, and even Gentiles bought offerings at the Jewish Temple and purchased lodging, food, and other necessities. While Galileans lived off the land, many Judeans were sustained by Temple worship.

Hakola continues his analysis, pointing out:

> The point of departure is the
> separation of different usages of the
> term [Jew] in John: many scholars
> note that sometimes it refers to
> the authorities in a hostile way,

> sometimes to the crowd in a more
> neutral way, and sometimes to
> different [positive] Jewish customs
> and festivals. (ibid, p. 12)

The important thing the reader must know about "the Jews" is the context in which it is used and whether the gospel writer means Jews from Judea, Jews from Galilee, a particular group of Jews within a greater crowd, such as Jewish authorities, or Jews in general.

The danger of reading a gospel text that reads, "The Jews..." is an oversimplification of the group without regard to the intra-Jewish dynamics described in the preceding paragraphs. Using such passages as a free pass to demonize Jews has allowed many other people-groups, even Christians, to participate in terrorizing and killing Jews throughout the world. Hitler used Scripture to justify genocide:

> A scholarly consensus arose that,
> though the Nazi project itself was not
> religiously based, it could not have
> spread as it did without the anti-
> Jewish foundations that were laid in
> Christianity's earliest literature and
> theology." (Azar, 2016)

The "normal" Christian would never sanction Nazi atrocities by citing gospel verses, but many Christians, like any other religious group, look for reasons to feel superior to other groups. This human failing was addressed in the "Stereotypes" chapter. Because of the unfathomable horror of Nazi actions, some have found either open or secret escape by comforting themselves with those gospel verses that imply Jews are the arch-enemies of Jesus. Perhaps it's easier to assuage the horror by telling one's self, "Well, if they hadn't been so mean to Jesus, they wouldn't be cursed. It was unfortunate for the Jewish people, but it's bound to happen."

This is simply not the case. Yeshua's work was not rejected by every Pharisee or Jew; in fact, Jews and Pharisees were chosen to carry the message to the Gentiles. Azar, a scholar who specializes in the Gospel of John, writes that people are inclined to forget that "...the gospel's authors were Jewish, that Jesus was Jewish, that the earliest followers were Jewish, and that the whole portrayal [in John's Gospel] was essentially an inner-Jewish debate."[72] Azar writes that with this historical knowledge, one can:

> ...throw scholarly weight against previous assertions (especially under the Third Reich) that the gospel was somehow the account of 'Jesus/ John against Judaism,' 'Christianity against Judaism,' or, perhaps worst of all, 'Gentiles against Jews.' ...the harsh rhetoric contained within the Fourth Gospel was not only a product of an inner-Jewish debate, but a normal inner-Jewish debate (by first-century standards).

The Gospel of John, when read in its original historical and social context, is not anti-Semitic or anti-Jewish. While on the surface, it appears that Yeshua argues with Jews in general, contextual reading lets the specific group of Jews among the whole take the credit or blame for the contention. Even some of the early Church Fathers, such as Origen, who were hostile to Jews, admit this and object to categorizing all Jews as "children of your father, the devil."

> Against Heracleon, Origen contends that no one can be a 'child of the devil' (cf. John 8:44) by nature; rather, looking to 1 John 3, Origen asserts that whoever commits sin has become of the devil: 'Insofar as we commit sins, we have not as yet

72. ibid

put off the generation of the devil,
even if we are thought to believe in
Jesus... [and] to the extent that he
has not yet destroyed the works of
the devil in us...we have not as yet
put aside being children of the devil,
since it is our fruits that show whose
sons we are.' (ibid)

This is only a small example from Christian scholarship's answer to the question of whether the gospels give anyone permission to equate Jews with the devil or look the other way because they are cursed. Paul, a Pharisee of Pharisees, argues that the Jews are beloved, and their partial blindness as to the identity of the Messiah is a Divinely-ordained necessity in order for the full number of Gentiles to come into the fold of Yeshua. Paul fully expects that once the fold is full, the blindness will be removed, and the Jews will be "resurrected" in their faith.

Perhaps Paul knew that few Gentiles would accept a fully Jewish Messiah, for across cultures, there has always been suspicion, hatred, and jealousy of Jews. There are many bumper stickers that read "My Boss is a Jewish Carpenter," but there are few that read, "My Messiah is a Jewish proto-rabbi who ate kosher, prayed in synagogues, was never convicted of any violation of Jewish law, and will rule with a rod of iron as the Lion of Judah."

The Father in Heaven sent forth a Messianic call to the nations. Many embrace both Messiah Yeshua and his Jewishness. Others read and embrace the New Testament as if God were mistaken in choosing Abraham, Israel, and the Jewish people, so Jesus came to fix God's mistake, shed his own Jewishness, and replace the beloved Israel with Christianity.

What if that second embrace is not borne out by an impartial, scholarly reading of the New Testament? Paul writes that this salvation process is a loop designed to close eventually. Jews will embrace Yeshua as Messiah in faith, and Christians will recognize Yeshua in his original context in faith. In fact, the Book of Revelation cannot be understood apart from Jewish law and tradition.[73] Yeshua will be a Lamb to the righteous of all races, but a ferocious Lion of Judah to the unbeliever. If the gifts of blessing on the Jew blessed the Gentiles *before* this reconciliation, then just imagine how much more the blessings *after* reconciliation!

Paul writes to the Romans:

> I say then, they did not stumble so as to fall, did they? May it never be! But by their transgression salvation has come to the Gentiles, to make them jealous. Now if their transgression is riches for the world and their failure is riches for the Gentiles, how much more will their fulfillment be!

> But I am speaking to you who are Gentiles. Inasmuch then as I am an apostle of Gentiles, I magnify my ministry, if somehow I might move to jealousy my fellow countrymen and save some of them. For if their rejection is the reconciliation of the world, what will their acceptance be but **life from the dead**? If the first piece of dough is holy, the lump is also; and if the root is holy, the branches are too.

> But if some of the branches were broken off, and you, being a wild olive, were grafted in among them and became partaker with them of the rich root of the olive tree, do not be arrogant toward the branches; but if you are arrogant, remember

73. See *Creation Gospel Workbook Two* and *Creation Gospel Workbook One* (The Seven Assemblies of Revelation) by the author.

that it is not you who supports the root, but the root supports you. You will say then, "Branches were broken off so that I might be grafted in." Quite right, they were broken off for their unbelief, but you stand by your faith. Do not be conceited, but fear; for if God did not spare the natural branches, He will not spare you, either.

Behold then the kindness and severity of God; to those who fell, severity, but to you, God's kindness, if you continue in His kindness; otherwise you also will be cut off. And they also, if they do not continue in their unbelief, will be grafted in, for God is able to graft them in again. For if you were cut off from what is by nature a wild olive tree, and were grafted contrary to nature into a cultivated olive tree, how much more will these who are the natural branches be grafted into their own olive tree?

For I do not want you, brethren, to be uninformed of this mystery—so that you will not be wise in your own estimation—that a partial hardening has happened to Israel until the fullness of the Gentiles has come in; and so all Israel will be saved; just as it is written, THE DELIVERER WILL COME FROM ZION, HE WILL REMOVE UNGODLINESS FROM JACOB. THIS IS MY COVENANT WITH THEM, WHEN I TAKE AWAY THEIR SINS.
From the standpoint of the gospel they are enemies for your sake, but from the standpoint of God's choice

they are beloved for the sake of the fathers; for the gifts and the calling of God are irrevocable.

For just as you once were disobedient to God, but now have been shown mercy because of their disobedience, so these also now have been disobedient, that because of the mercy shown to you they also may now be shown mercy. For God has shut up all in disobedience so that He may show mercy to all.

Oh, the depth of the riches both of the wisdom and knowledge of God! How unsearchable are His judgments and unfathomable His ways! For WHO HAS KNOWN THE MIND OF THE LORD, OR WHO BECAME HIS COUNSELOR? Or WHO HAS FIRST GIVEN TO HIM THAT IT MIGHT BE PAID BACK TO HIM AGAIN? For from Him and through Him and to Him are all things.

To Him be the glory forever. Amen. (Ro 11:11-36)

**And amen.**

# 9

## THE HEAVY YOKE

> They [scribes and Pharisees] tie up
> heavy burdens and lay them on
> men's shoulders, but they themselves
> are unwilling to move them with so
> much as a finger. (Mt 23:4)

Although is it impossible in a booklet to explain all the dialogues between Yeshua and different sects of Jews, one debate concerns the "heavy yoke," and it is fairly easy to understand. In the First Century, the obligations of the Jewish people to their covenant was called "the yoke of the Torah." Moses assured the Israelites in the wilderness that the commandments he passed on to them in the Torah were not too difficult to do: "For this commandment which I command you today is not too difficult for you, nor is it out of reach."[74]

Even in the Book of Leviticus, with all its detailed rules and regulations about ritual and personal purity, Adonai assures the Israelites: "So you shall keep My

74. Dt 30:11

statutes and My judgments, by which a man may *live* if he does them; I am the LORD."[75]  The key is that the commandments are something that enliven a person who is walking in his faith.  The only death built into a Godly commandment is its inherent righteousness which may "kill" a human being's untamed soul that strives against obedience.

In this sense, believers do take up their crosses daily, for as Origen pointed out in the previous chapter, a believer's sinful nature still arises from time to time.  If the individual chooses to obey the commandment over self-will, there is a virtual "death," but it is ultimately for resurrected life.  A commandment was never given to make one literally die.

The First Century reality of a practicing Jew is difficult to imagine.  Three times per year, he had to travel to Jerusalem to worship at the Temple.  As long as the Temple stood, there were rules of ritual purity that had to be respected before one could enter into the holier courts and offer sacrifices.  It was a higher level of purity than one practiced in everyday life, and there are many *mikvaot*[76] in the Temple area where people could immerse themselves for ritual purity before entering the Temple.

Personal purity in home practice was also a consideration, but not so onerous.  Many people, however, went above and beyond the letter of the law, choosing stone jars instead of clay[77] to hold large volumes of water.  Clay had to be destroyed if a dead lizard or some other unclean thing fell into it, but other substances, like stone or metal, could pass through water or fire and be pure again.

Although this sounds difficult, modern culture is typically very scrupulous with personal hygiene and cleaning containers.  For instance, an American will think twice before placing a plastic container in a dishwasher, for it could melt.  A metal container is safe.  Learning the Levitical laws about vessels was

75. Le 18:5

76. ritual baths, what Christians call "baptismals"

77. The water that Yeshua turned into wine in Galilee was in stone jars, suggesting the owner was scrupulous about ritual purity...and wealthy.

not that difficult, especially if one were brought up practicing it in the home.

The easy yoke of the Torah became heavier when the high level of purity necessary for Temple visits was gradually imposed on the common Jew. Some scholars believe this was an imposition of the Pharisees and their fences. They believe that when a Jew refused the extra rules, the Sadducees and Pharisees labeled them as commoners, "Am Ha-Aretz," or People of the Land. It was not a compliment. While some believe that the derogatory phrase was reserved for Galileans, others say it applied to any Jew, commoner or priest, who rejected the additional fences of purity.[78] On the other hand, in some observances, Galileans were more scrupulous, for they did not work at all on the eve of Passover, while the Judeans worked until midday.[79]

Some attribute the extra "yoke" rules to the Sadducees, who dominated the priesthood and Temple responsibilities. Charlesworth writes:

> In contrast to the Pharisees who were
> relatively lenient and who seem
> to have demanded purity rulings
> only for the Temple's precincts,
> many of the Jerusalem priests and
> Sadducees, who were genuinely
> and rightly zealous about purity,
> tended to demand of all Jews the
> holiness once required of only priests.
> During the First Temple period, the
> high priest was a religious officer. In
> the Second Temple period, he also
> became a powerful political leader.
> (p. 395)

One may question this since the Sadducees in general were not enthusiastic about extra rules. Regardless, disputes over the increasing purity rules arose, and the New Testament reader becomes increasingly

78. Kittel, Bromiley & Friedrich, p. 20

79. Klausner, p. 326

confused and annoyed with them as much as the Am Ha-Aretz! The Pharisees did, however, know the difference between routine hygienic cleanliness and ritual purity either in the home or Temple. They did not confuse the two. According to the Babylonian Talmud (Hullin 10a), hygienic cleanliness holds a higher place than ritual purity because the danger of disease or sickness outweighs prohibitions of impurity.[80]

In Judea and Lower Galilee, Jews felt the encroachment of the requirements for ritual purity beyond the requirements of the Torah. Archaeologists are finding many *mikvaot* for ritual immersion and stone vessels, throughout Lower Galilee and Judea in almost every Jewish city, village, and town.[81] These objects testify to the yoke that was growing heavier in those regions.[82] Yeshua's very Galilean Jewish answer was that it was too much. This created even more animosity from those who controlled Temple worship.

Jews in the Upper Galilee, such as Yehuda NaNasi, had a good relationship with Rome. This brought suspicion upon them from the Judeans, who hated the Romans and their occupation of their holy city. Galileans viewed the Judeans as political extremists or religious fanatics.

If Yeshua's disciple Judas was a Zealot as is thought, it makes Judas' alliance with the school of Shammai logical. Judas would have frowned upon Yeshua's opening the altars to Gentiles in the Temple by overturning the moneychangers' tables. He would have not identified with some of the Galilean disciples, who proved they were "Am Ha-Aretz" by not ritually washing their hands before eating. This would have been done in the Temple, but was not required by the Torah itself outside of the Temple. The home table did not have to equal the purity of eating the holy things offered in the Temple.

80. Charlesworth, p. 397

81. "The obsession with ritual purity had spread to the Lower Galilee, for a recent archaeological discovery in Reina, Israel, uncovered a quarry for chalkstone, which was used for plates and cups. According to the Torah and rabbinic understanding, although pottery easily contracted ritual impurity from dead bugs and such, and therefore had to be broken, and metal vessels had to be immersed to purify them, stone vessels retained ritual purity." (Eisenbud, August 10, 2017).

82. Ibid, p. 406

The Pharisees and some of the scribes gathered around Him **when they had come from Jerusalem**, and had seen that some of His disciples were eating their bread with impure hands, that is, unwashed. (For the Pharisees and **all the Jews** do not eat unless they carefully wash their hands, thus observing the traditions of the elders; and when they come from the market place, they do not eat unless they cleanse themselves; and there are many other things which they have received in order to observe, such as the washing of cups and pitchers and copper pots.) The Pharisees and the scribes asked Him, 'Why do Your disciples not walk according to the tradition of the elders, but eat their bread with impure hands?' (Mk 7:1-5).

Charlesworth notes that "some of Jesus' disciples did wash their hands and most importantly, so did Jesus; otherwise his antagonists would have made Jesus' noncompliance their central attack."[83] This passage helps to illustrate the point of differentiating which "Jews" are present in a given text. The text says, "all the Jews." How can it be "all the Jews" when those who failed to wash their hands were also Jews? The writer assumes the reader understands the context.

First, the Pharisees and scribes have "come from Jerusalem," which is Judea, the more extremist region of the Jewish population. The reader surmises that the challengers are feeling the weight of coming "from Jerusalem," and their awareness is heightened, for Jews in Judea were very scrupulous about ritual washing.

Regular, widespread use of ritual

83. p. 426

baths and chalkstone vessels was not at all unique to Jerusalem or the priesthood, but rather was commonplace to a comparable degree in Jewish society throughout early Roman **Judea**. Jews everywhere throughout the country strove on a regular basis to maintain the purity of their bodies, clothing, utensils, food, and drink, and there is no reason to suppose that in doing so they somehow had the Temple in mind. This new understanding encourages us to reinterpret the archaeological finds from Jerusalem as reflecting an important facet of **prevailing common culture**... (Adler, 2016, pp. 228-248)

The Judean Jews were particularly scrupulous in their observance, so what was less uniform in the Upper Galilee was routine in Judea. These are the "all Jews" of Mark Seven.

It is obvious that Jews know the difference between washing for hygiene and washing for ritual purity. Under the influence of Hillel's successors, later Talmudic rabbis document that hygienic washing is of greater importance than ritual washing. Even the average Jew was conscious of ritual purity, but the snoops wanted to impose their interpretation and application upon everyone. This is not a human phenomenon isolated to Pharisees, Sadducees, or Jews!

Mark also mentions "the washing of cups and pitchers and copper pots." In the Jewish law, there is a section called *Kelim*, meaning "Vessels." There are extensive instructions (30!) concerning the purity of vessels in that section alone. It's easy to see why the more independent Am Ha-Aretz weren't interested in endless details of ritual-washing, which was not a rejection of the written Word, but the "heavy yoke" descending upon them from those who controlled Temple worship far away in Jerusalem.

An Am Ha-Aretz did not have to mean someone from the Galilee. It was a term used to describe those who rejected the additional purification rules issuing from the Temple leadership. Even after the destruction of the Temple, the Galilean Am Ha-Aretz were not completely within the fold of rabbinic Judaism until the second half of the second century.[84]

For Yeshua and other Jews facing purity legislations not found in the Hebrew Bible, these multiplied regulations were undermining the ability of the average Jew to be considered pure. It's not that they were impure according to the written Word, but by the standard of "the elders" in Jerusalem. Charlesworth suggests that the high priests sent allies from among the scribes and Pharisees from Jerusalem to other regions to monitor their new purity enactments. They questioned those who came to worship in Jerusalem, for there is something common in those narratives:

> Jesus is opposed by those who
> control the Temple and demand
> an acceptance of their own
> interpretation of the tradition of the
> elders. Such rifts in Second Temple
> Judaism were not new; rejection of
> those who control the Temple cult
> and who interpret Torah incorrectly is
> clear in documents composed after
> the Babylonian Exile, and especially
> around 150 BCE. (pp. 407-408)

Maintaining this ritual purity was rigorous even for those of the lineage who grew up learning how to prepare for Temple service. The imposition of this same rigor upon the merchant, carpenter, farmer, or fisherman was heavy. While one may engage in

84. Kittel, Bromiley & Friedrich, p. 33

scrupulous observance, taking on the yoke of priestly ritual purity was not demanded by the Scriptures. In fact, such a high standard is nearly impossible considering the everyday demands of a secular job.

Ironically, remnants of this heavy yoke survived the destruction of the Second Temple.  The Temple could no longer host the ritual copies that Moses had viewed in their perfection,[85] yet the words and the pattern of the Torah were preserved in Jewish homes.  By making the consciousness of ritual purity a reality to the layman, those vital Bible precepts continued to be remembered and guarded in transition Judaism.

Although the yoke was too heavy for many, and the Sadducees disappeared with the destruction of the Temple, the Pharisees ensured that the Temple practices were never forgotten after its destruction. Purity rituals such as hand-washing before meals and viewing one's dining table as a metaphor of the Temple altar endure to this day in Jewish homes. Because the Pharisees conditioned the Jewish people to practice personal purity and faithfulness, the Temple continued to be the symbol that tied them together no matter where they were scattered and exiled in the world.

In summary,

85. Ex 25:9

86. This is not to diminish the heart-changing power of the Holy Spirit, which transforms commandments into love, not drudgery or rote actions.

a) the "heavy yoke" was extra rules that were not enjoined in the written Word; Yeshua represented the "easy yoke" promised by Moses to the Israelites[86]

b) many Judeans voluntarily took on this heavy yoke

c) those who rejected the Temple authorities' extra rules were called Am Ha-Aretz

d) archaeology documents that many Galileans also went the extra mile to maintain ritual purity

e) the term "Jews" must always be read with regard to sectarian and regional context in the gospels

There have always been challenges to Jewish traditions from outsiders who perceive them as counterproductive to spiritual freedom or insincere. Periodic challenges also came from great scholars with Judaism itself, Yeshua and his Galilean disciples being an early example. Rabbi Abraham Kook, a giant of Judaism at the turn of the 20th Century wrote these words:

> Tradition is a moment in the endless flow of eternity, wrenched from the whole and given shape and form that permits us to continually re-encounter it. But at the same time, it distracts us from new light pressing on us. Tradition is precious as far as it goes, but it helps to keep us in the confinement of finitude. (Kook, 1978, p. 4)

While tradition can provide the safety of fences that prevent transgressing the actual written Word, the danger is that it can prevent the community from encountering the Light of the Torah in transforming new ways. The fence may be mistaken for the written Word, and Yeshua preached that the tradition is always "lighter" than the "heavier" Word. That which is heavy in importance is a lighter yoke.

# 10

## PAUL, THE FADING PHARASEE

A bit of history concerning the last days of the Second Temple is helpful in understanding Paul, the traditional proto-rabbi preaching to Gentiles. For a more in-depth history of the transition from the Pharisees of the First Century to the rabbinic period following, see S. Creeger's *Introduction to the Jewish Sources*. Paul was one "late-born," meaning that although he was contemporary to Yeshua's first disciples and apostles, he was born later, and he could see Jewish history changing before his eyes.

Paul's death occurs just prior to the destruction of the Second Temple, so surely Paul the Pharisee could see "the writing on the wall," the impending destruction prophesied by Messiah Yeshua. The Temple buildings would be completely destroyed, leaving only the retaining walls underpinning the Temple Mount.

The other Pharisees could see it as well. While Jerusalem was under siege by the Romans, a famous sage, Rabbi Yochanan ben Zakkai (a student of Hillel), was concealed in a coffin and carried out of the city by his students. Outside of the walls of the city, he emerged from the coffin and requested an audience with the commanding officer. He surrendered himself to Vespasian and prophesied that Vespasian would be made Caesar.

Vespasian was pleased with such a prophecy, which was later fulfilled, so Yochanan ben Zakkai requested permission take his students and start a yeshiva[87] in Yavneh. He asked for the family of Rabbi Gamaliel to be spared (Gittin 56b). The Gamaliel family was a respected Pharisaic dynasty descended from Hillel, and the reader will remember that Paul studied with a rabbi named Gamaliel, who was part of this scholarly family:

> I am a Jew, born in Tarsus of Cilicia, but brought up in this city, educated under Gamaliel, strictly according to the law of our fathers, being zealous for God just as you all are today. (Acts 22:3)

Here is a list of "princes" from the Gamaliel family until the end of the Mishnaic period, that is, until the beginning of the third century CE:

> 1. Gamaliel the Elder (Gamaliel I), first half of the first century.
>
> 2. Simeon ben Gamaliel (Simeon ben Gamaliel I), son of (1).
>
> 3. Gamaliel of Yavneh (Gamaliel II), son of (2).
>
> 4. Simeon ben Gamaliel (Simeon ben Gamaliel II), son of (3).
>
> 5. Judah the Prince, editor of the

87. Jewish religious school

128

Mishnah, son of (4).

6. Gamaliel (Gamaliel III) son of (5).

It was likely the grandson of Hillel, Gamaliel II, who advocated for Peter and the other apostles when the Sadducean chief priests wanted to kill them for preaching Yeshua's resurrection:

> ...they were cut to the quick and intended to kill them. But a Pharisee named Gamaliel, a teacher of the Law, respected by all the people, stood up in the Council and gave orders to put the men outside for a short time. And he said to them, 'Men of Israel, take care what you propose to do with these men. For some time ago Theudas rose up, claiming to be somebody, and a group of about four hundred men joined up with him. But he was killed, and all who followed him were dispersed and came to nothing. After this man, Judas of Galilee rose up in the days of the census and drew away some people after him; he too perished, and all those who followed him were scattered. So in the present case, I say to you, stay away from these men and let them alone, for if this plan or action is of men, it will be overthrown; but if it is of God, you will not be able to overthrow them; or else you may even be found fighting against God.' (Acts 5:33-39)

In 70 C.E. the walls of Jerusalem were breached and the Second Temple was destroyed. The Jews were prohibited from living in Jerusalem, so the remaining rabbis moved to Yavneh. It was from there that the transition from the proto-rabbinic Pharisaic period to the rabbinic period of Jewish history took place. The more compassionate rulings on the applied Torah from the House of Hillel prevailed over the more stringent ones from the House of Shammai, and the Oral Law, which had been preserved orally from rabbi-to-student, eventually was recorded in the *Mishnah*.

Paul surely understood that Jewish life for his generation was about to change, and some of that fatalism is expressed in his letters.[88]

> But perceiving that one group were Sadducees and the other Pharisees, Paul began crying out in the Council, 'Brethren, I am a Pharisee, a son of Pharisees; I am on trial for the hope and resurrection of the dead!' (Acts 23:6)

In this proclamation, Paul unapologetically proclaims his religious affiliation. He is not being hypocritical, but instead identifying what, to him, is the most important thing to know about the Pharisees: they have hope in the resurrection of the dead. Paul doesn't say, "I *was* a Pharisee," he says, "I *am* a Pharisee!" To Paul, the identification of Pharisee is synonymous with a belief in the resurrection of the dead to either eternal reward or punishment. In that sense, Christians are also Pharisees!

Paul always felt that "Pharisee" described his doctrinal approach to the Scriptures, not just the single topic of the resurrection from the dead. He writes:

88. See *Creation Gospel Workbook Three: Spirit-filled Family* for an analysis of Paul's letter to the Corinthians.

> If anyone else has a mind to put confidence in the flesh, I far more: circumcised the eighth day, of the nation of Israel, of the tribe of Benjamin, a Hebrew of Hebrews; as

to the Law, a Pharisee (Philippians 3:5-5)

Paul brings up an old rabbinic argument. When should a new convert be circumcised? The Jerusalem Council in Acts considered the question because it was no longer a matter of a few people, but large numbers. One school of rabbinic thought advocated circumcising immediately, which would weed out those who were insincere and merely experimenting with religion. Others said immersion in water was more important to a new convert.[89]

Another school of thought said no, that's not the way. A pagan yesterday, and a Jew today, just because he's circumcised? No. A convert must be taught at least the basic Scriptures and become competent in them before he starts running around telling people he's Jewish! Mere circumcision doesn't turn a polytheist into a practicing Jew. Some rabbis thought that a potential convert must accept all of Jewish law before he was accepted for conversion. [90]

Paul was all for circumcision when it involved Timothy, who had been taught the Scriptures from a young age and who was expected to minister to other Jews. In circumcision, Paul exercised a Pharisaic approach to solving the problems and questions based on the individuals involved.

Paul was also a Roman citizen, a status which he didn't mind using a few times as recorded in the Book of Acts.

> But when they had stretched him out for the whips, Paul said to the centurion who was standing by, 'Is it lawful for you to flog a man who is a Roman citizen and uncondemned?'

89. Klausner, 1989, p. 246

90. Telushkin, p. 35, and Falk, p. 17 & 19

The Zealots of the First Century sometimes viewed the

Pharisees as "smoothies,"[91] a sect who tried to make peace with the Romans or other foreign entities for the peace to study free of harassment. The example of Yochanan ben Zakkai, who negotiated escape and a learning center with Vespasian, illustrates how the Pharisees were able to accept the impending destruction of Jerusalem long before the Zealots, who killed other Jews whom they feared would surrender to the Romans.

According to one historian, this made the Pharisees "anti-nationalist," but in their view, it made them realists. As Yeshua prophesied, the day was coming when the Temple and Jerusalem would no longer function as the center of Jewish worship, and the services would have to migrate into local synagogues and the home. This practice is illustrated in early Nazarene Judaism, in which Jewish believers both worshiped in the Temple at the appointed times and gathered in local synagogues, yet they also attended special gatherings of like-minded believers. By the late period of Yeshua's generation (53-54 AD), Paul writes:

> Do you not know that you are a
> temple of God and that the Spirit of
> God dwells in you? (1 Co 3:16)

91. Eisenman, p. 38
Paul was preparing First Century believers to see themselves as mobile temples, for soon the Jerusalem Temple would be destroyed. This was not anti-nationalism, but Pharisaic realism. The Pharisees' acceptance of impending political and religious change was not popular;[92] it was the Zealots who preached the message of resistance and victory over Rome[93] that the people wanted to hear. Discerning one's time, however, is important. Continuity as a people depended upon the Jews' ability to hold tightly to their ancient and eternal heritage, the Scriptures.

92. ibid, p. 46

93. See The Seven Shepherds: Hanukkah in Prophecy by the author for an explanation of Messianic prophecy related to Rome.

94. Mt 22:21

Because the Pharisees were willing to work with the

Roman governing authority to ensure that schools of learning could continue, they survived the destruction of Jerusalem and much of Judea. Paul the Pharisee urged similar behavior upon the Gentile converts, going so far as to say that governing authorities are God-appointed:

> If it be possible, as much as lieth in you, live peaceably with all men. (Ro 12:18 KJV)

> Let every soul be subject to the governing authorities. For there is no authority except from God, and the authorities that exist are appointed by God. (Ro 13:1 NKJV)

> Render to all what is due them: tax to whom tax is due; custom to whom custom; fear to whom fear; honor to whom honor. (Ro 13:7)

> Remind them to be subject to rulers and authorities, to obey, to be ready for every good work... (Titus 3:1 NKJV)

No one would expect Paul to mean that a believer should deny Messiah or commit a gross transgression of the Word if an authority demanded it, but in daily life, there was no reason to antagonize ruling forces. This willingness to cooperate allowed a measure of freedom to continue walking in one's faith rather than bringing swift annihilation such as Jerusalem experienced only a few years after Paul's death. Yeshua paid his taxes,[94] and he called a tax collector to be his disciple, going even beyond the Pharisees who may have paid taxes, but they shunned the tax collectors.[95] Likewise, Peter, who was not known to be a Pharisee, acknowledges in a very Pharisaic way:

> Honor all people, love the

95. Even Yeshua shunned tax collectors [Mt 17:18] like unconverted Gentiles (Sanhedrin 25b), for they incurred defilement in a house, so those with whom he interacted or called must have exhibited a willingness to 1) abandon skimming excessive fees before handing the money over to the Romans: "And some tax collectors also came to be baptized, and they said to him, 'Teacher, what shall we do?' And he said to them, 'Collect no more than what you have been ordered to.' [Lk 3:12-13] or to 2) listen to and follow his teaching of repentance [Lk 18:13]. There's a difference between honoring the position of an unrighteous authority and becoming friends or mixing with it. Neither Yeshua nor the Pharisees went so far as to mix with Rome.

brotherhood, fear God, honor the
king. (1 Pe 2:17 NKJV)

Once he corrected his Messiah identification
problem, Paul the Pharisee was the perfect choice
of an emissary to the Gentiles. Because of his Hillelite
Pharisaic training, he:

- was willing to teach and convert
  Gentiles into Jewish faith
- could work within the ruling Gentile
  governmental establishment
- confidently proclaimed the resurrection
  of the dead and judgment, both
  reward and eternal punishment
- From the Fading Pharisee to the
  Rabbis of the Mishnaic Period

When the Second Temple was destroyed, the *bat kol,*
or heavenly voice, announced a path for Jews after
the destruction of the Temple in 70 CE. According to
Jewish sources, the Temple was destroyed because
of "baseless hatred" among brothers. This booklet
has identified some examples of those conflicts, such
as the murder of Hillel's students while Hillel approved
by not voicing objection. The final chapter of
brotherly hatred is very similar.

> After the destruction of the Temple, the rabbis reflected:
>
> **Why was the *first* Temple destroyed?**
>
> ▼ Because of three things: idol worship, sexual immorality and murder.
>
> **But the *second* Temple, when the people were engaged in the study of Torah and fulfilled the commandments and performed acts of kindness, why was that destroyed?**
>
> ▼ Because of sinat chinam, baseless hatred.
>
> From this we learn that sinat chinam is considered equal to the three sins of idol worship, sexual immorality, and murder. (Yoma 9b)

"Baseless hatred" is a simple summary of why the Second Temple was destroyed, but for those interested in the "Old Lady Who Swallowed the Fly" version, the Talmud explains the inciting event and a summary of the story. Although Yeshua prophesied it would occur, the series of events trace all the way back to Yeshua's overturning of the moneychangers' tables. Yeshua and the Hillelites objected to Shammai and the Sadducees' repudiation of Gentile converts and Gentile sacrifices in the Temple.

The First Temple was designed by King Solomon to accommodate proper sacrifices brought by Gentiles, and every Feast of Tabernacles, seventy bulls were offered during this "Feast of the Nations," celebrating a time when the Prophets foresaw the nations coming to Jerusalem to worship. Instead, Shammai looked the other way when the Temple authorities found ways to take the Gentiles' money for sacrifices and divert it to other Temple funds.

The story started with a simple case of mistaken

identity:

> The destruction of Jerusalem came through a
> Kamza and a Bar Kamza in this way. A certain man
> had a friend named Kamza and an enemy named
> Bar Kamza. He once made a party and said to his
> servant, "Go and bring Kamza."
>
> The man went and brought Bar Kamza. When the
> man [who gave the party] found him there he
> said, 'See, you tell tales about me; what are you
> doing here? Get out.'
>
> Said the Bar Kamza 'Since I am here, let me stay,
> and I will pay you for whatever I eat and drink.'
>
> The man said, 'I won't.'
>
> 'Then let me give you half the cost of the party.'
>
> 'No,' said the other.
>
> 'Then let me pay for the whole party.'
>
> He still said, 'No,' and he took Bar Kamza by the
> hand and put him out.
>
> Said Bar Kamza, 'Since the Rabbis were sitting
> there and did not stop him, this shows that they
> agreed with him. I will go and inform against them,
> to the Government.' He went and said to the
> Roman Emperor, 'The Jews are rebelling against
> you.'
>
> The Emperor said, 'How can I tell?'
>
> Bar Kamza said to him: 'Send them an offering and
> see whether they will offer it on the altar.'
>
> So the Emperor sent with him a fine calf. While on
> the way, Bar Kamza made a blemish on its upper
> lip, or some say, on the white of its eye, in a place

> where Jews count it a blemish, but Gentiles do not.
>
> The Rabbis were inclined to offer it in order not to offend the Government. Said Rabbi Zechariah ben Abkulas to them: 'People will say that blemished animals are offered on the altar.' They then proposed to kill Bar Kamza so that he should not go and inform against them, but Rabbi Zechariah ben Abkulas said to them, 'Is one who makes a blemish on consecrated animals to be put to death?'
>
> Rabbi Johanan there upon remarked: 'Through the humility of Rabbi Zechariah ben Abkulas, our House has been destroyed, our Temple burnt, and we ourselves exiled from our land.' (Gittin 55b - 56a)

The implication is that the rabbis, who were the spiritual leaders, should have spoken up at the party and entreated the host for peace. By remaining silent, they were perceived by the humiliated Bar Kamza as sanctioning the humiliation. Bar Kamza sets up the rabbis with the very mercy they have preached, but failed to practice in a crucial moment. They preached:

- Who is honorable? One who honors his fellows. (Pirkei Avot 4:1)
- Do not scorn any man, and do not discount any thing. (4:3)
- One who...humiliates his friend in public...although he may possess Torah knowledge and good deeds, he has no share in the World to Come." (3:11)

It was a pivotal moment in history. Death and destruction followed that resounding silence to a brother's offense. In the Roman siege, Jewish zealot killed Jewish brother. The Temple was destroyed by the offended Emperor. The Emperor was provoked by one offended brother, who sparked the destruction of the Temple and murder and enslavement of hundreds of thousands of Jews, his own brothers and sisters. Even the similarity in the name confusion tells a story. As the Apostle James sagely said, "How great a matter a little fire kindles."

Following the destruction of the Temple and the dispersion of the Jews into foreign lands, the Pharisees faded from history. Judaism entered a period known as rabbinic Judaism centered in local synagogues. The Hillelites prevailed, and a more homogenous practice of Judaism was practiced in local synagogues.

It was over a hundred years after the destruction of the Temple that the Oral Law was written and preserved as a guideline for rabbis to teach their students orally. Just as the appearance of Pharisees cannot be exactly determined, neither can the exact moment of their transition to rabbinic Judaism. For a concise history of this period, review S. Creeger's BEKY Booklet entitled *Introduction to the Jewish Sources*.

The doctrinal and teaching heritage of the Pharisees passed on to generations that would develop Jewish law, custom, and tradition into such works as the Talmud and *Shulchan Arukh*. The simpler First Century study of the Oral Law that passed from rabbi to student became comprehensive, and schools of study called *yeshivot* multiplied and spread.

# 11

## ME? A PHARISEE?

The entire theology of the New Testament Scriptures rests on the doctrines developed by the Pharisees from the ancient text of the Bible:

- Encourage a righteous life by making the Scriptures understandable to all, regardless of birth, wealth, or social standing
- The resurrection of body and soul, slung away in eternal punishment, or rewarded to dwell in the Kingdom of Heaven.

For Jew or Gentile who believes this message of Yeshua and accepts him as the Messiah sent to accomplish this, Yeshua makes a place, tying him or her into the bundle of the living.

There are a few problems that readers of the New Testament can experience:

- They are not equipped to understand the defining eschatological beliefs of different

groups that engaged in conversations with Yeshua, to differentiate Jew from Jew.
- They are not equipped to understand the differences in eschatological and practical applications of beliefs among *like-minded* groups that engaged in conversations with Yeshua.
- They are saddled with an inherited scorn for Judaism, and therefore Jews, in general. Ethnocentrism and stereotyping.

The Pharisees had neither horns nor halos. They were just people. Some were sincere, others insincere, and probably many were in-between, just like most religious groups. If all Pharisees were mean, greedy, and hypocritical, then how did they win the hearts of the masses? People look for religious leaders who are examples and who live according to the most ideal expression of the faith. The fact that Yeshua called out the greedy and hypocritical individuals validates the existence of the pious ones like Nicodemus.

Modern fiction, drama, media, and even politics thrive on a frenzy of emotion. Viewers, readers, and voters need increasing doses of anger, rage, relief, and righteous indignation to function in daily life. We look for villains and arch-enemies, for the social and religious holding-pens of Good and Evil, Red and Blue, Winner and Loser need to be filled each day. The Scripture is not written in such a way, though. Scripture invites its readers to exercise intelligence and apply its lessons to one's own life:

> All scripture is given by inspiration of God, and is profitable for doctrine, for reproof, for correction, for instruction in righteousness: that the man of God may be perfect, thoroughly furnished unto all good works. (2 Ti 3:16-17 KJV)

The gospel lessons are for its readers' personal

correction and growth in righteousness. Scriptural history invites readers to consider that sometimes Pharisees are good and Samaritans are bad.

Messiah Yeshua is not Luke Skywalker. If Messiah is Messiah, then he does not need a convenient evil empire to make him so or to make his story a blockbuster and bestseller. It is mankind's sin that killed the Lamb. All mankind. If one accepts Yeshua's salvation, then it makes no sense to seek someone else to blame. The sooner that the sinner repents of greed, meanness, and hypocrisy, the sooner grace will cover her or him.

Rather than place all Pharisees into boxes in which they don't fit, those who study Yeshua's life can be thankful that the Pharisees set the stage of Messianic expectation among First Century Jews. That expectation prepared the way for Yeshua to preach, heal, die, and resurrect. Eventually, he will take his role in punishment, judgment, and rewards at the resurrection of the dead. Beliefs about Pharisees may have been inherited, but it is time to think upon things about them that were lovely. The perception of Pharisees has too long been skewed, and there is much about their brief history for which to be grateful.

Friendly Gifts of the Pharisees:

- Faith in the spirit, soul, and bodily resurrection of the dead
- Faith in a final judgment and reward or punishment
- Faith that the righteous non-Jew has a portion in the World to Come on a par with the native-born Jew
- The rabbinic theological point of view from which the Book of Revelation is written
- A desire to make the Word understandable to everyone, regardless of wealth, intelligence, or social status

- Willingness to "start slow" teaching Gentiles

But what about...?

No doubt you have many textual challenges racing through your mind about Yeshua's negative conversations with the Pharisees. Some of these are addressed in *Truth, Tradition, or Tare: Growing in the Word*. For a head start, contextualize the "foe" situations:

- Which specific "Jews" or "Pharisees" are involved?
- What are the beliefs of that particular group?
- Is Yeshua addressing *motivations* rather than *practices*, something not unique to Pharisees but all people who desire to be set-apart and study the Scriptures? Some do it for self-glory, some for God's glory.

Am I a Hypocrite?

Yeshua points out traits that are "leaven" among the Pharisees. A Pharisee is someone who believes in the resurrection of the dead, reward or punishment for earthly deeds, a Messiah, angels, and guidelines to hold a faith community together (based upon the written Word). In that sense, most Christians are Pharisees! They are not, however, Jewish by birth, but grafted in. Christians can still learn from the lessons Yeshua preached to the Pharisees and the lessons they preached to themselves:

> Don't be hypocrite, practicing your faith like an actor. Do live your faith sincerely.

> Don't do things to skirt the written Word. Do uphold the written commandments.

> Don't do religious things to gain the
> attention and approval of people.
> Do be humble.

> Don't use the Word to prove
> yourself superior to others. Do learn
> something from everyone.

Isn't there irony in the fact that these principles are taken from the Pharisees' Oral Law?[96] Bible readers are very familiar with the leavening agents of personal faith, and all are guilty of transgressing in his or her worst moments. We have all been sincere, insincere, and so sincerely leavened! The challenge is to clean out the leaven in one's personal walk.

Yeshua's disciples were not warned against Pharisees, but against their *leaven*: pride and hypocrisy.[97] Yeshua taught Bible readers many of the Pharisees' applications of the Word. Before the Pharisees faded from history, the Kamza-Bar Kamza example taught a powerful lesson:

> Don't remain silent when you have
> the power of reconciliation. Do
> speak up when it is possible to
> reconcile brothers.

Because the Pharisees were on the world stage for a tiny window of time, Yeshua extended *the lesson* of the Pharisees to future generations. To those who have received great spiritual riches, especially teachers of the Word, much is required. Sincerity. Humility. Kindness. Generosity. The leavened Pharisees were a departure from the Pharisaic ideal.

Yeshua gives an example:

> But they do all their deeds *to*
> *be noticed by men*; for they
> broaden their phylacteries [*tefillin*]
> and lengthen the tassels of their

96. Pirkei Avot

97. Lk 12:1. In Mark 8:15, Yeshua also speaks of the leaven of Herod. His listeners would know what kind of "leaven" Herod was practicing and what would characterize the leaven of a Pharisee.

garments. (Mt 23:5)

In Hebrew, phylacteries are *tefillin*, and wearing them is commanded in the Torah. The Talmud indicates in Megillah 24b that by the time of its writing, primarily Jewish believers in Yeshua wore round phylacteries or decorated them with precious metals, and they wore them "without scruple."[98] The Jewish believers didn't believe that Yeshua's criticism of certain Pharisees' broad tefillin negated the written commandments in Deuteronomy 6:8 and Exodus 13:16 to wear them. Those who did not follow Yeshua wore square-box tefillin.

Yeshua rebuked the practice of enlarging the tefillin and lengthening *tzitziyot* (tassels) so that others would see it and think the wearer more pious. Yeshua did not negate the fulfillment of the written Word. There is a big difference between condemning the fulfillment of a commandment and condemning the *motivation* behind keeping it. Archaeology provides insight as to what a normal-sized tefillin was.

The phylacteries found by archaeologists at Qumran are crafted with the four compartments found in modern tefillin, but they have more of a rectangular shape in the photos. They are small, averaging only about 2-3 centimeters long and 1 centimeter wide. Tefillin in Yeshua's day weren't just small, they were tiny! This allowed those men who wanted to wear them throughout the day to do so like a headband. Some probably did so because they loved the Word so much; others did it to be perceived as pious.

Yeshua knows the heart.

Some Christians wear crosses or Bible verses as jewelry, or they put bumper stickers and fish symbols on their cars because they love Yeshua so much. Some probably do so in order to be perceived as pious.

98. Bagatti, 1984, p. 101

Yeshua knows the heart.

Figure 6 - Qumran Tefillin (open and enlarged).
Actual size was much smaller.

Figure 7 - Tefillin Closed

The First Century tefillin were designed to be part of the individual's daily life. No big deal. Nothing elaborate.

There ´ is a fine line between doing acts of righteousness, kindness, and obedience that bring glory to the Holy One and doing them to bring approval and attention to ourselves. Do social media today, or back in the "good ol' days," church signs, ever make a shocking statement or Scripture proclamation that really isn't designed to bring people to repentance? Instead, it glorifies one's own interpretation, good works, or better standing with the Father? Worse yet, is it taunting sinners? Do believers seek personal approval from other people using Scripture or obedience as the lure? This is by Yeshua's definition the leaven that was found among some Pharisees.

One might say, "I'm just proclaiming the Word. It's not self-serving, but God-serving." Don't forget, Yeshua knows what is in people's hearts regardless of their proclamations and long, public prayers. Soul searching is a personal responsibility. In fact, if believers took their frustrations over enemies of their faith to prayer first, then it's likely most of it would never end up on the broad boxes and long tassels of social media. Do believers or teachers of the Word really need to post provocative things copiously on social media to boost their "likes" or "follows"? Is it all done to "reach" people? And if so, for what...or whom?

Yesterday's broad tefillin have become today's attention-getting broadcasts. It more likely that influencing people with one's steady, workday faith will grow more fruit than a hundred billboards or a thousand internet posts.

This is another area where believers in Yeshua can learn from history and the Pharisees:

> Nevertheless, many even of the rulers believed in Him, but because of the Pharisees they were not confessing Him, for fear that they would be put out of the synagogue; for **they loved the approval of men rather than the approval of God**. (Jn 12:42-43)

The synagogue of Shammai ruled in the time of Yeshua's adulthood. Their strict interpretations and exclusiveness were at odds with Yeshua's more graceful, Hillel-type rulings. Some of Hillel's students had even been murdered over doctrinal disputes. There were leaders in Judea who believed in Yeshua's message, but they feared being put out of their synagogues more than they loved him. Under pressure, even Simon Peter denied knowing Yeshua, and the other disciples ran away.

While some denied Yeshua because they wanted people's approval more than his, it is possible to do the same by using Yeshua's Word to convince ourselves that we are standing up *for* him. In reality, we stand up for him to gain attention and approval from other people, not draw them close to Yeshua. The "evil eye" that Yeshua preached against was not just stinginess; in that historical period, it meant displays of personal success or actions to attract attention and admiration from others. Multiplied social media today make believers susceptible to becoming attention-seekers, insatiably and greedily acquiring "views" and "engagements." Be prayerful about what needs to be said or posted publically so that it does not become leaven.

There are other abuses of a disciple's calling. Many believers reprove others for some omission or difference in their observance of Scripture when their own lives are riddled with omissions or mis-applications. Hasn't everyone had an issue on which she or he just "knew" she was right, but in time, the facts proved that the belief was wrong? This is the scary part: it feels just the same to be wrong as it feels to be right! A human being can be completely convinced that he is right when he is completely wrong.

How many times will someone at work criticize a co-worker for being habitually late when he or she habitually gossips, makes personal calls, or surfs the internet on company time? The hypocrisy is even more troubling when it invades relationships among people of shared faith in the God of Abraham, Isaac, and Jacob.

There is no small irony that those who so blithely call someone else a Pharisee are frequently oblivious to their own leaven. Yeshua uses such an example in a parable in which the Pharisee compares himself in prayer to a tax collector. While the Pharisee busily draws attention to the tax collector's sins, and then to himself and his piety, something a normal Pharisee would not do, the tax collector practices the Pharisaic custom of beating the breast and refusing to look up while he says a confessional prayer. He's talking directly to God, not onlookers.

The tax collector is the *real, unleavened* Pharisee of the story, upholding the principles of the Pharisaic doctrine of personal humility. The leavened Pharisee thinks he is justified in his public prayer, bringing glory to God, but he isn't. May our own proclamations and public posts be as humble and repentant before the Father as the tax collector's, and may our humility not be cunningly public to elicit serial sympathy. The tax collector wasn't looking around to see who was watching his heartfelt confession.

It's not that we can't share our successes and failures with others; there are times that we should as a personal testimony of Adonai's mercy and wisdom. It's the *purpose* to which we share them. Some things should be reserved for close family and trusted friends. Yeshua was selective in what he shared with whom. He was spied upon frequently upon by leavened scoffers, so he chose not to teach the deeper wisdom indiscriminately. He knew that it would multiply the mockers and give fuel to their fires, so sometimes he withheld the fuel. Because Yeshua was judicious with his words and approval audience, there was a multitude of sins never committed.

Another challenge is to quit scapegoating Pharisees. Although today a Pharisee is synonymous with a religious hypocrite, one cannot ignore the hatefulness and mass murder of Jews that it has justified through the centuries.

What can you and I do? Perhaps it's simply taking the word "Pharisee" out of our vocabulary when it doesn't concern a gospel discussion. Maybe it's explaining the stereotype to others who are using the word in ignorance. By all means, never post or forward derogatory cartoons and other smug religious comments using "Pharisee" or "Jew" on social media. It is tempting because it points out religious hypocrisy, but then again, do Yeshua's disciples want the character of the *real* Pharisee, the tax collector in repentance for his own failings, or the *leavened* Pharisee, who is preoccupied with others' failings?

It has nothing to do with being politically correct, but being Biblically sensitive to our Jewish brothers and sisters. Social and print media can be terrible hammers that embed Jewish stereotypes deeply. It is hard to dig them out even when one has better information. If one feels compelled to expose "leaven," remember that Yeshua used examples of leaders in his generation. The listeners understood the examples. Our examples, too, must relate to leaven that our generation understands instead of demonizing ones that they don't.

All beginnings are hard,[99] but if not now, when?[100]

99. Rashi to Exodus 19:5

100. Hillel

# QUESTIONS FOR REVIEW

1. Define a Pharisee according to its use in the Hebrew Bible.

2. What role does community play in the life of a Torah-observant person?

3. Define the Pharisaical schools:

   a. What were the two groups of Pharisees?

   b. Who were their leaders?

   c. What were their differences?

4. What were the differences between Pharisees and Sadducees?

5. List the challenges of the "Three Gentile Converts":

#1_____.

#2_____.

#3_____.

6. What are the dangers of stereotyping?

7. Give examples of Yeshua's "fences" around the Torah:

#1_____.

#2_____.

#3_____.

8. Why was Paul so bold in proclaiming himself a Pharisee?

9. Read the passage below, and list the Pharisaical doctrines you can find:

And he said to me, 'Do not seal up the words of the prophecy of this book, for the time is near. Let the one who does wrong, still do wrong; and the one who is filthy, still be filthy; and let the one who is righteous, still practice righteousness; and the one who is holy, still keep himself holy. Behold, I am coming quickly, and My reward is with Me, to render to every man according to what he has done. I am the Alpha and the Omega, the first and the last, the beginning and the end. Blessed are those who wash their robes, so that they may have the right to the tree of life, and may enter by the gates into the city. Outside are the dogs and the sorcerers and the immoral persons and the murderers and the idolaters, and everyone who loves and practices lying. I, Jesus, have sent My angel to testify to you these things for the churches. I am the root and the descendant of David, the bright morning star.' (Re 22:10-16)

#1_____.

#2_____.

#3_____.

#4_____.

#5_____.

#6_____.

10. "Just at that time some Pharisees approached, saying to Him, 'Go away, leave here, for Herod wants to kill You.'[101] Why would Pharisees want to protect Yeshua?

101. Lk 13:31

# ADDITIONAL READING

Alewine, H. 2016. *Truth, tradition, or tare: growing in the Word.* London, KY: BEKY Books.

_____. 2016. *What is the Torah?* London, KY: BEKY Books.

Beutler, J. 2001. "The Identity of the 'Jews' for the Readers of John." Pages 229–39 in Anti-Judaism and the Fourth Gospel. Edited by Reimund Bieringer, Didier Pollefeyt, and Frederique Vandecasteele-Vanneuville. Assen: Van Gorcum.

——— . 2000. "'The Jews' in John's Gospel: Fifteen Years of Research (1983–1998)."
Ephemerides theologicae lovanienses 76: 30 – 55.

——— . 2001. "'You Are of Your Father the Devil' in its Context: Stereotyped Apocalyptic Polemic in John 8:38–47." Pages 418–44 in Anti-Judaism and the Fourth Gospel. Edited by Reimund Bieringer, Didier Pollefeyt, and Frederique Vandecasteele-Vanneuville. Assen: Van Gorcum

Charlesworth, J. & Johns, L. (1997). *Hillel and Jesus: comparative studies of two major religious leaders,* Minneapolis: Fortress.

Creeger, S. (2016). *Introduction to the Jewish sources: preserving history, structure, and heart.* London, KY: BEKY Books.

Schaper, J. *The Pharisees in The Early Roman Period,* edited by W. Horbury, W. D.
Davies– J. Sturdy, The Cambridge History of Judaism, vol. 3, Cambridge: CUP, 1999, 402-427; see esp. 407

Von Wahlde, U. (1982). "The Johannine 'Jews': A Critical Survey." New Testament Studies 28: 33 – 60.

# REFERENCES

Adler, Y. (2016). Between priestly cult and common culture. *Journal of Ancient Judaism, 7*(2).

Azar, M. (2016). Stereotyping exegesis: The Gospel of John and "the Jews" in ancient and modern commentary. In *Exegeting the Jews* (Brill, April, 2016). Retrieved September 2016 from http://www.bibleinterp.com/articles/2016/09/aza408014.shtml)

Bagatti, B. (1984). *The Church from the Circumcision: history and archaeology of the Judaeo-Christians.* Jerusalem: Franciscan Printing Press.

Ben Malka, O. and Shahar, Y. (2015). "Returning: reflections and resources on T'shuvah." Selected readings from *A Damaged Mirror: a story of memory and redemption*, supplemented with Jewish sources. Alfei Menashe, Israel: Kasva Press.

Berryhill, J. (1999). *Women restored.* Ontario: Essence Publishing.

Biblical Studies Press. (2006). *The NET Bible First Edition Notes* (Jn 1:19). Biblical Studies Press.

Bredin, M. (2003). *Jesus, revolutionary of peace: A nonviolent Christology in the Book of Revelation.* Milton Keynes: Paternoster.

Charlesworth, J. *The Temple, purity and the background to Jesus' death.* RCatT XXXIII/2 (2008) 395-442. Academia.edu. Retrieved 10/12/16 from https://www.academia.edu/28891918/The_Temple_purity_and_the_Background_to_Jesu s_Death

Cohn, H. (1971). *The trial and death of Jesus.* New York: Ktav Publishing.

Dalman, G. & Lightfoot, J. (2002). *Jesus Christ in the Talmud and commentary on the Gospels from the Talmud and the Hebraica.* (R. Parrish, Ed.). Eugene, OR: Resource Publications.

Edersheim, A. (1994). *Sketches of Jewish social life*. Peabody, MA: Hendrickson Publishers.

Eisenbud, D. (2017, August 10). Archeologists find 2,000-Year-Old rare stone vessel used in Jewish rituals. August 10, 2017. *The Jerusalem Post*. Retrieved 11/8/18 from http://www.jpost.com/Israel-News/Archeologists-unearth-2000-year-old-stone-vessel-production-center-502056

Eisenman, R. (1998). *James, the brother of Jesus*. New York: Penguin.

Elliott-Binns, L. (1956). *Galilean Christianity*. London: SCM Press, Ltd.

Falk, H. (1985). Jesus the Pharisee: a new look at the Jewishness of Jesus. Eugene, OR: Wipf and Stock Publishers.

Fishbane, M. Isaiah 40-66: Return and restoration. *My Jewish Learning*. Retrieved 9/3/18 from https://www.myjewishlearning.com/article/isaiah-40-66-return-and-restoration/

Gillman, N. (2015). *The death of death: resurrection and immortality in Jewish thought*. Woodstock, VT: Jewish Lights Publishing

Gold, A., Ed. (2018). *The complete Artscroll Selichos*. (Y. Lavon, Trans.). New York: Mesorah Publications, Ltd.

Hakola, R. (2005). *Identity Matters: John, the Jews and Jewishness*. Boston: Brill.

Holladay, W. L., & Köhler, L. (2000). *A concise Hebrew and Aramaic lexicon of the Old Testament* (111). Leiden: Brill.

Klausner, J. (1989). *Jesus of Nazareth: His life, times, and teaching*. (Hebert Danby, Trans.). New York: Bloch Publishing Company.

Kook, A. (1978). *The Lights of penitence, the moral principles, lights of holiness, essays, letters, and poems*. (Ben Zion Bokser, Trans.). New Jersey: Paulist Press.

McCleod, S. (2007). Maslow's hierarchy of needs. *Simply Psychology*. Retrieved 6-25-17. https://www.simplypsychology.org/maslow.html

G. Kittel, G. W. Bromiley, & G. Friedrich, (Eds). Pharisaism from its beginning to the fall of the hierarchy in Jerusalem. *Theological dictionary of the New Testament*. (Vol. 9). (electronic ed.) (13). Grand Rapids, MI: Eerdmans.

Raphael, S. (2009). *Jewish views of the afterlife*. (2d Ed). New York: Rowman and Littlefield Publishers, Inc.

Saldarini, A. (2001). *Pharisees, scribes, and Sadducees in Palestinian society: a sociological approach*. (electronic ed.). Grand Rapids, MI: Eerdmans.

Telushkin, J. (2010). *Hillel*. New York: Schocken Books.

Torrance, I. (2006). *In comical doctrine: An epistemology of New Testament hermeneutics*. Milton Keynes: Paternoster.

Troost-Kramer, K. (2016, November 13). Jesus and his fences around the Torah. *Israel Study Center*.

Schunat Even Yisrael. (1995). *Schunat Nachlaot*. Jerusalem: Ulpan-Or.

Utley, R. (2003). Luke the historian: The book of Acts. (Vol. 3B). *Study Guide Commentary Series*. Marshall, TX: Bible Lessons International.

# ABOUT THE
# AUTHOR

**Dr. Hollisa Alewine** has her B.S. and M.Ed. from Texas A&M and a Doctorate from Oxford Graduate School; she is the author of Standing with Israel: A House of Prayer for All Nations, The Creation Gospel Bible study series, and a programmer on Hebraic Roots Network. Dr. Alewine is a student and teacher of the Word of God.